T0323072

The Diaspora and Returnee Entrepreneurship

The Diaspora and Returnee Entrepreneurship

Dynamics and Development in Post-Conflict Economies

Nick Williams

OXFORD
UNIVERSITY PRESS

Oxford University Press is a department of the University of Oxford. It furthers
the University's objective of excellence in research, scholarship, and education
by publishing worldwide. Oxford is a registered trade mark of Oxford University
Press in the UK and certain other countries.

Published in the United States of America by Oxford University Press
198 Madison Avenue, New York, NY 10016, United States of America.

Library of Congress Cataloging-in-Publication Data
Names: Williams, Nick, 1977– author.
Title: The diaspora and returnee entrepreneurship : dynamics and
development in post-conflict economies / Nick Williams.
Description: New York, NY : Oxford University Press, [2021] |
Includes bibliographical references and index.
Identifiers: LCCN 2020027032 (print) | LCCN 2020027033 (ebook) |
ISBN 9780190911874 (hardback) | ISBN 9780190911898 (epub)
Subjects: LCSH: Entrepreneurship. |
Economic development. | Return migration.
Classification: LCC HB615.W5523 2021 (print) |
LCC HB615 (ebook) | DDC 338/.0408691—dc23
LC record available at https://lccn.loc.gov/2020027032
LC ebook record available at https://lccn.loc.gov/2020027033

DOI: 10.1093/oso/9780190911874.001.0001

1 3 5 7 9 8 6 4 2

Printed by Integrated Books International, United States of America

Contents

Acknowledgements

Writing a book is time-consuming. As such, I owe thanks to my employer, the University of Leeds, for making the time available to do so. I am also extremely grateful to the financial support of the Leverhulme Trust Research Fellowship scheme (grant no. RF-2016-297), which provided me with a valuable investment in my time and resources to enable the research on which much of this book is based to be carried out.

I would also like to thank all of the entrepreneurs, policy makers, and other stakeholders who have taken time to be interviewed or who have taken part in surveys for the research included in this book. Without their willingness to participate, the research and this book would not have been possible.

I am also very grateful to those who have assisted me in facilitating access to entrepreneurs, policy makers, and stakeholders within Bosnia and Herzegovina, Kosovo, and Montenegro, and for providing me with numerous insights into the research. Many thanks to (in alphabetical order): Jasmina Ahmetbasic, Abetare Domi, Adnan Efendic, Liza Gashi, Besnik Krasniqi, Bernard Nikaj, Dragana Radevic, Berat Rukiqi, Linda Tahiri, and Ruzmira Tihić-Kadrić. The research was infinitely improved through their assistance.

I am also grateful to the many colleagues who have inspired me in this research over the years, especially those who have commented on chapters or ideas contained within the book and who helped me formulate my ideas. Thanks to (in alphabetical order): Tamer Cavusgil, Adnan Efendic, Mariana Estrada Robles, Isla Kapasi, Besnik Krasniqi, Emmanuella Plakoyiannaki, and Friederike Welter.

Lastly, this book is dedicated to Alex, Emily, and Holly. Alex and Emily, you are funny and wise, and have made this journey much, much more enjoyable. Remember: life moves pretty fast; if you don't stop and look around once in a while, you could miss it. Lastly, Holly, thank you. You changed everything.

1

Between Isolation and Assimilation

Understanding the Diaspora and Returnee
Entrepreneurship

> Sometimes we feel that we straddle two cultures;
> at other times, that we fall between two stools.
> —**Salman Rushdie (1992)**, *Imaginary Homelands:*
> *Essays and Criticism 1981–1991*

1.1. Introduction

This book analyses the role that the diaspora play when returning as entrepreneurs to their homeland. Returnee entrepreneurs are defined as individuals who have moved away from their home country and have lived as part of
the diaspora, and later returned home to live, invest, or both. With increased
movements of people around the world, the role of transnational economic
activity is becoming ever more significant. Large-scale outward migration
has long been an element of global economic development, from early movements out of Europe to the New World, to dislocation created by the World
Wars, and recent migration to Europe from Africa following the Arab Spring.
Furthermore, recent conflicts in Syria and Ukraine have placed forced migration in sharp focus, with receiving countries developing approaches to
manage and absorb new waves of migrants.

Migration is a global phenomenon and people are moving across international borders more than ever before. The United Nations (2020) estimates that there are now around 272 million international migrants, and
that this has grown from 173 million at the turn of the millennium. Global
migration has lifted millions out of poverty and has boosted economic
growth, with people often moving in search of new opportunities unavailable to them at home. Migrants can triple their wages after moving to a
new country, which has helped millions of individuals and their relatives
at home escape poverty (World Bank, 2018). Receiving countries gain the

The Diaspora and Returnee Entrepreneurship. Nick Williams, Oxford University Press (2021). © Oxford University Press.
DOI: 10.1093/oso/9780190911874.003.0001

skills and talents of new migrants. Developed countries with welcoming immigration policies gain the most: the United States, the United Kingdom, Canada, and Australia are home to almost two-thirds of migrants with university-level education; and the United States has 85% of all immigrant Nobel Science Prize winners (World Bank, 2018).[1] Also, at lower levels of skills and qualifications, countries benefit: migrants fill critical roles, for example in construction, agriculture, and healthcare. As Greenspan and Wooldridge (2018, p. 346) state in relation to the United States, immigration has 'allowed business to gorge on human capital—cheap labour for the fast-food restaurants and skilled labour for Silicon Valley'. Yet of course managing migration is not without its challenges. New waves of migration create issues of integration, meaning that effective policy responses are required (Collier, 2015). Infrastructures for accepting migrants are required, as well as policies to ensure that when migrants reach their destination they have access to healthcare, housing, and education or employment. In addition, not all migration is in search of new opportunities. People also move to escape conflict, poverty, and persecution. The United Nations High Commissioner for Refugees (UNHCR) estimates that 71 million people have been forcibly displaced worldwide (UNHCR, 2019). This amplifies the challenges of integration. Often those displaced by conflict have had to move quickly, leaving behind homes, jobs, as well as sometimes family and friends. Thus finding opportunities upon arrival in the country that they move to can be difficult.

Much of the research on migration focuses on the host country, that is, the country migrants move to. Yet less is known about what happens later, when people decide to return to their homeland. Indeed, Gamlen et al. (2017) state that migration research has tended to focus more on immigration policies by destination states rather than emigration policies made by the migrants' country of origin. Thus the notion of return requires focus. Why do people return to their homelands after living away? Do relative changes in economic opportunity between different countries drive return, or are other motivations more prevalent? This book explores these issues of return, illuminating motives and linkages with the homeland of people who have moved away, and then seek to return. The book examines this return in the context of entrepreneurship, examining the entrepreneurial opportunities at home compared to the host country.

---

[1] Although the United States has been moving away from its reputation as a welcoming destination for all under the immigration policies of President Trump; while the United Kingdom's 2016 Brexit vote to leave the European Union was in part explained as a reaction against the free movement of people.

International entrepreneurship as an area of scholarly inquiry dates from Oviatt and McDougall's (2005) study of international new ventures, to recent calls for consideration of the diversity of context and action (Reuber et al., 2018). Many migrants engage in entrepreneurial activities; however, these individuals have been largely peripheral in mainstream discourses on entrepreneurship (Ram et al., 2008). An emerging body of literature has begun to explore the experiences of such entrepreneurs (Koning and Verver, 2013; Lin et al., 2018). Yet despite this work, understanding the role and contribution of outward and return migrants to entrepreneurship and economic development still requires attention (Li et al., 2012).

The emergent research recognises that the diaspora are attractive as a resource for home country development. The diaspora gain advantages through international experience, access to education, and work experiences abroad. They can then use this experience and their knowledge of home contexts if they return. Those individuals who are alert to opportunity are able to harness these advantages for individual and societal gain. Just as people can move away from home due to perceived superior economic opportunity abroad, so too can people return when economic conditions improve. For example, studies have focused on the 'sea turtles' who have been attracted to return to China after moving abroad for work or study (Qin et al., 2017).

Exploiting opportunities at home is not simply a result of an individual's alertness, skills, and experience. It is also largely dependent on the institutional context in which the opportunity occurs. In fast-growing economies, opportunities are manifold. Yet in more challenging contexts, opportunities are fewer and more constrained. Such economies provide valuable lessons for academic discourse and public policy as they typically have turbulent and underdeveloped institutional environments. Such environments present challenges for economic actors within the country, and also for the individual returnee entrepreneur in navigating the institutional environment. Yet it also represents a huge opportunity for those countries able to harness their diaspora given that they can contribute to the economy through their skills, international experience, and investment, and can bridge entrepreneurial gaps at home. In recognition of this, migrant-sending and receiving governments are grappling with competing priorities, interests, and options encompassed in diaspora policy (Brinkerhoff, 2012, 2017). Indeed, there has been a growth of formal national policy frameworks aimed at harnessing the diaspora, with diaspora-focused policies now operational in over half of the United Nations' member states (Gamlen et al., 2017).

Much of the extant research on returnee migration focuses on large, dynamic, fast-growing economies (see, for example, Drori et al., 2009; Qin and Estrin, 2015; Li et al., 2017; Pruthi et al., 2018). In these contexts, entrepreneurs can return to take advantage of multiple and multiplying opportunities in developing markets, utilising the expertise and knowledge they have gained abroad. Returns to smaller, less developed economies, where their expertise may be more difficult to directly apply, is under-researched. The 'sea turtles' are returning to China to fill managerial gaps at home, but the application of expertise to more complex environments is less clear. In addition, little is understood about the dynamics of returnees among those who have been 'forced' to move. Instead of moving because of superior opportunity abroad, individuals may be forced to move because of, for example, war, famine, or natural disasters (Joireman, 2017; Williams and Krasniqi, 2018).

This book focuses on the return of international entrepreneurs to post-conflict economies. Economies under conflict experience significant outward migration, as well as ongoing economic and social challenges following the cessation of violence. This often leaves them with a large diaspora, who are able to contribute to their homeland when violence has ended, if they see that there are opportunities at home or they want to contribute to reconstruction and development. Among this diaspora are entrepreneurs who can return and play a potentially key role in their home country. This book focuses on these returnee entrepreneurs: those who were forced to move because of conflict and are now returning to their homeland to work, live, and/or invest. It draws on empirical evidence from the post-conflict, newborn countries of Bosnia and Herzegovina (hereafter B&H), Kosovo, and Montenegro. The fall of the former Yugoslavia led to widespread conflict across the Balkans during the 1990s. This tumultuous period saw B&H, Kosovo, and Montenegro all suffer the direct effects of violence; and a lasting legacy has seen prosecutions associated with crimes against humanity and genocide continue to 2017 through the International Criminal Tribunal for the former Yugoslavia. The wars also led to widespread emigration, with people moving in order to avoid conflict. Each country now has a sizeable diaspora community spread around the world, as well as the challenge of a developing weak economy. Positive institutional reforms have been slow to develop, creating numerous challenges for entrepreneurs and limiting economic growth. Given that entrepreneurship is generally regarded as a productive force for change in the development of modern economies, this promise also holds for post-conflict economies. Attracting returnee entrepreneurs home offers one route towards improved economic development.

1.2. Context Matters

It has become well established in the entrepreneurship literature that context matters (Welter et al., 2017a). Returns to different forms of entrepreneurship are sensitive to institutional contexts (Estrin et al., 2016). Institutions structure the incentives to which individuals respond, based on the information they have available (North, 1990). Thus, the institutional environment determines if people engage in productive, unproductive, or destructive activities (Baumol, 1990). Institutions can embody formal political rules that set out legal action and responsibility, while modes of exchange, norms, and values are inherently informal (Bylund and McCaffrey, 2017). Both the formal and informal interact with individual decision-making and influence choices regarding action (Ahlstrom and Bruton, 2002). Where the institutional environment rewards productive behaviours, economic development can be secured.

The interaction of formal institutions (defined as the rules and regulations which provide the economic and legal framework of societies) and informal institutions (defined as the unwritten codes of conduct, norms, and values that define societies) is crucial in fostering entrepreneurial activity (Williams and Vorley, 2015). While the literature on institutions and entrepreneurship in transition economies is well established, institutional development in post-conflict states is less understood. In these economies, without institutional stability and improvements even the most experienced diaspora entrepreneurs may be discouraged from investing.

While institutions have previously been studied in isolation, it is the interaction between the formal and the informal that is crucial. Where the formal and informal complement each other, entrepreneurial activity will be fostered; conversely where there is asymmetry or a lack of complementarity between the two, entrepreneurial activity will be held back. Williamson (2000) demonstrates how institutions operate at different levels and influence each other, with informal institutions often emerging spontaneously but influenced by the construction of formal rules. As such, formal rules are mediated by interaction with informal norms, and the economic outcomes of these change over time (Winiecki, 2001). It is therefore not sufficient for policy makers to simply consider the formal rules when trying to foster entrepreneurship. Every formal institutional change will impact informal institutions. And every adjustment of informal norms and values will influence the effectiveness of formal institutions. Ensuring the complementarity or alignment of formal and informal institutions is of critical importance.

Studies of transition economies have shown how institutions have seen 'path extension', with previous institutional arrangements adapted and re-defined with varying degrees of success. For many this has meant a focus on improving formal institutions, with changes in informal institutions being slow to emerge (Estrin and Mickiewicz, 2011). However, the institutional environment of post-conflict economies studied in this book can be under-stood as having experienced 'path break' and subsequently new 'path cre-ation' as a result of the formation of newborn states (Williams and Vorley, 2017). In these economies, creating institutions which can foster entrepre-neurship, and with it deliver socio-economic development and transforma-tion in post-conflict environments, represents a particular challenge. There are immediate issues associated with embedding and enforcing newly estab-lished formal institutions, while in path dependence terms the extension of prevailing informal institutions simultaneously serves to undermine these reforms due to the substitutive effect. For entrepreneurs in post-conflict en-vironments, navigating new formal institutional frameworks can be chal-lenging. Efendic et al. (2015) note that in such economies, where the social fabric has been damaged, the level of trust is low and people are unwilling to share knowledge, which then serves to further stymie entrepreneurial endeavours.

Clearly these challenges are faced by entrepreneurs within the country. Yet navigating such institutional environments is even more challenging for returning entrepreneurs who may never have lived in the home country, or who know relatively few people in the country (Nielsen and Riddle, 2010). Weak institutional environments can also lead to negative perceptions among returnees who view the financial risk to investments, lack of sup-port, political fragmentation, and weak institutional framework as barriers to investment (Agunias and Newland, 2012). Yet returnee investment does occur, even in the most complex institutional environments. Returnees are able to harness their international experience by connecting formal net-works of businesses, as well as informal networks of family and friends, across borders (Elo, 2016), allowing them to develop knowledge of the in-stitutional environment. Such networks enable returnees to overcome the 'liability of foreignness' associated with outside investment (Zaheer, 1995). Returnees can overcome the liability by becoming (re)connected with local constituents and developing understanding of the institutional changes at home (Li et al., 2012).

1.3. Embeddedness across Borders

Migrants who have lived for a long time in a host country often maintain connections to their homeland. As such, they can be embedded across borders. For entrepreneurs, the returns to investment available in home and host countries will differ due to the divergent institutional environments. They can thus use their embeddedness in different economies to benefit their activities across borders.

It is important at this stage to note a key difference in the analysis contained within this book from those of other authors. Scholars such as Jennifer Brinkerhoff (2016, p. 45) focus on the notion of 'institutional entrepreneurs' defined as 'people who, typically along with others, help transform an institution: introducing new social or cultural or cultural forms/logics into the world.' Such institutional entrepreneurs are embedded within their home country. This book, however, focuses on the interactions of individuals *within* institutional environments. The diaspora can be embedded in more than one location and can compare the relative payoffs of different places. It thus offers insights regarding how institutions shape entrepreneurial activity, rather than focusing on how entrepreneurs seek to change the institutional environment themselves. Indeed, this book shows that often entrepreneurs will pursue strategies that avoid engagement with institutional change possibilities.

Brinkerhoff (2016) has written eloquently and expertly on the 'in-between advantage' of the diaspora. In Brinkerhoff's analysis, diaspora entrepreneurs are able to influence and change institutions in their home country, and can act as 'change agents' (Riddle and Brinkerhoff, 2011; Kshetri, 2013). However, this book reveals the challenges of being a change agent in post-conflict contexts. The book shows that when entrepreneurs return to challenging environments they can seek to avoid institutional challenges rather than try to change or influence them. They are familiar with the culture and context at home, which can encourage investment (Leblang, 2010), but also understand the barriers associated with influencing the policy landscape. Returnee entrepreneurs are not necessarily seeking to change institutions through their actions. Rather, their actions are the outcome of navigating the institutional environment. In this way, the individual returnee is focused on entrepreneurship and investments *within* the existing institutional framework. The institutional framework affects whether individuals elect to pursue entrepreneurial activity, including influencing returnee entrepreneurs.

The book demonstrates that the diaspora communities of post-conflict economies are often caught between 'isolation and assimilation'. They can be isolated because of their years living abroad, as well as their negative perceptions of the institutional environment at home. Yet many of them also wish to become more assimilated and have an emotional desire to help their home country. Many stay away and do not invest. Many of those who returned soon after independence left again due to the institutional challenges, becoming isolated again. Those who returned later, following perceived institutional improvements, have sought to avoid the negative impact of barriers to entrepreneurship, and can for example avoid government engagement activities as they mistrust policy actors' intentions. By investing at home they can diversify their business portfolio, maintaining investments in their host country as a way of insuring themselves against the risks inherent in the challenging environments at home. Others will return to live and invest, with their attachment to home providing an impetus to overcome the problematic institutional environment. They therefore do not become truly assimilated at home as they avoid government engagement activities and this impacts their long-term investments.

The notion of 'isolation and assimilation' demonstrates that embeddedness across borders has differential impacts on the individual. In this sense, it highlights that entrepreneurship is a socialised process (Drakopolou Dodd and Anderson, 2007) and that there is a relationship between the entrepreneurial self and society (Jack and Anderson, 2002). Context influences the perceptions of entrepreneurs, and embeddedness across borders recognises different and changing social norms, perceptions, and values, as well as the different opportunities available. Although many government policies are seeking to assimilate the diaspora, in post-conflict economies this has so far been less than fully effective.

1.4. The (Potential) Benefits of Returnee Entrepreneurship on Development

Despite the importance ascribed to entrepreneurship in the economic development process (Acs et al., 2008), the role of returning entrepreneurs is less understood. Wright et al. (2008) argue that constraints on entrepreneurship in a country could be offset by return migration of skilled entrepreneurs. Many fast-growing economies, for example India and China, have seen the return of the diaspora in response to increasing opportunities (Li et al., 2012). Yet as Qin and Estrin (2015) state, little is known about the factors and mechanisms which influence the diaspora to launch, or invest in, entrepreneurial activities at home. This is despite the fact that these diaspora entrepreneurs may have great potential to contribute to economic growth, as well as reconstruction and development in post-conflict economies.

If one considers that among the diaspora community, there are entrepreneurs returning from work or education in a developed economy to their home country to start a new venture or invest in others, their potential appears undeniable. The diaspora can straddle different cultures, societies, and economies, drawing on different experiences to develop their human, social, and financial capital. This experience not only benefits the individual but also can benefit those in the homeland through the sharing of capital, applications of technical knowledge, and expectations of how business should be conducted, as well as direct investment in their own or other's entrepreneurial activities (Riddle and Brinkerhoff, 2011; Williams, 2018). Diaspora entrepreneurs can gain knowledge and skills that are lacking in their home country (Nielsen and Riddle, 2010). When they return to invest or start a new business, they remit this acquired human capital back to the origin country, thereby turning 'brain drain' into 'brain gain' (Saxenian, 1999; Stark, 2004). In order to contribute at home, diaspora entrepreneurs draw on their formal and informal networks between their country of origin and their host country. These allow knowledge to be transferred as well as trade to be developed. First-generation diaspora entrepreneurs can have strong informal networks at home, as they had relationships with native family and friends before emigrating, and more formal networks are built over time through business experience and success. Second-generation diaspora are able to develop networks through their family and friends, although their emotional tie to the homeland will be weaker. These networks can reduce the 'space' between countries and thus facilitate entrepreneurial activity.

In addition to these potential benefits, the diaspora can also contribute to their home country through remittances, defined as direct people-to-people money transfers between migrants and their relatives (Klekowski von Koppenfels, 2017; Zheng and Musteen, 2018). While this is not diaspora entrepreneurship per se, it can go towards supporting entrepreneurial activity at home. However, more commonly, remittances go towards supporting friends and family, and are an example of the diaspora feeling moral responsibility to benefit the development of their home country. The impact of remittances is debated, and research has moved beyond consideration of them as the key source of transfer from the diaspora (Clemens et al., 2014). Despite their large volumes, the benefit of remittances for economic growth is questionable. As much of it is in the form of household transfers, remittances can provide income that is often essential to sustenance but could be applied for a variety of purposes, including conspicuous consumption (Brinkerhoff, 2016).

In moving debates forward about the potential impacts of the diaspora, it is important to recognise that although much research posits the positive impacts of the diaspora, negative outcomes can also result. Just as entrepreneurship more broadly cannot be considered as a singular route for economic and social salvation (Blackburn and Ram, 2003) or as always inherently 'good' (Shane, 2009), neither is returnee entrepreneurship. Investments made by returnee entrepreneurs may not always be efficient and can crowd out domestic investment and displace local firms, reducing local competition, leading to lower quality products and inflated prices. Although emotional attachment is a motivating factor, sentiments of altruism can be a constraining factor, and some may invest for social status or for political gain (Elo and Riddle (2016). In addition, policy makers who view the diaspora as agents of change risk overlooking the potential of those who remain within their borders (Bakewell, 2008). Consequently, diaspora engagement should not be considered as a simple 'win-win' (Pellerin and Mullings, 2013), and for economies in need of investment and higher rates of entrepreneurship, as in post-conflict contexts, strengthening diaspora investment and entrepreneurship is important but not without challenges.

This book recognises the undoubted potential of diaspora entrepreneurs to benefit their homeland. Yet it also recognises the challenges in doing so. Not all diaspora entrepreneurship will be beneficial. Not all policy interventions will be effective, despite good intentions. Yet the lessons contained within this book are that by understanding the challenges and opportunities associated with diaspora entrepreneurship, more effective strategies can be put in place.

1.5. Return to Challenging Environments

Post-conflict economies provide a number of theoretical and policy implications in understanding returnee entrepreneurship. This book focuses on the Balkan economies where conflicts occurred in the 1990s, although there have been ongoing political tensions. Because of this, it is possible to analyse the longer-term impacts of forced migration and return, by comparing first- and second-generation migrants as well as policy trajectories. Also by examining these countries, implications can be developed for other economies currently experiencing high volumes of outward migration, whether through conflict or other impacts.

B&H, Kosovo, and Montenegro are all newborn, independent states created out of the violent break-up of the former Yugoslavia. All three are building institutions from unique starting points, rather than developing institutions from the past. Instead of adopting previous Yugoslavian socialist central planning, they are seeking to create open market-orientated economies. Each of the three countries have implemented varying versions of liberal economic reform, which has included significant privatisation of state assets (Knudsen, 2010; Williams, 2018). As such, they have had a 'path break' in their institutional arrangements as formal institutions, akin to what Acemoglu and Robinson (2012) define as critical junctures. Indeed, all three countries have experienced major disruption to their economic and political landscape due to conflict; despite this negative impact, it has created the potential for positive reform.

B&H declared independence from Yugoslavia in 1992. This precipitated a bitter ethnic war which ended in 1995, the legacy of which is a divided country with stark divisions between the predominantly Bosniak Federation and the Serb-dominated Republika Srpska. These divisions have made the co-ordination of effective policy difficult, meaning that B&H has failed to place itself on a path towards growth and development. Kosovo was previously part of Yugoslavia and then Serbia, and the war of 1998–1999 served to further damage its already fragile economy. Following the continuation of political and ethnic tensions after the end of the war, Kosovo unilaterally declared its independence as a newborn state in 2008, albeit with continued tensions in parts of the country. Montenegro was part of various Yugoslav and Balkan unions for many years and maintained political ties with Serbia following the collapse of Yugoslavia. However, growing differences led to a referendum vote for independence in 2006. As such, while Montenegro felt the effects of the Yugoslav wars, these were not as pronounced as in B&H and Kosovo; nevertheless, it has still seen significant emigration associated with the overspill of conflict and ongoing economic challenges.

As post-conflict economies, B&H, Kosovo, and Montenegro all face numerous obstacles to economic and social development, which have implications for policies targeting the returnees. The countries have all experienced high levels of unemployment and poverty, and low levels of growth, all of which have contributed to further migration. B&H's diaspora is estimated at approximately 2 million, equivalent to 53% of the population (MHRR, 2016); Kosovo's diaspora is estimated at approximately 700,000 people, equivalent to 40% of the resident population (United Nations Development Programme, 2014); and Montenegro's diaspora is estimated at 200,000, equivalent to 32% of the population (Government of Montenegro, 2014). While remittances from the diaspora became increasingly important following the war, each country is seeking more effective ways of harness their diaspora. Yet the book finds that policy is often uncoordinated, with national strategies not translating into direct policy. Improving the policy landscape, in particular the institutional environment, is crucial if these countries are to harness diaspora entrepreneurship.

As the book shows, the diaspora of B&H, Kosovo, and Montenegro hold strong ties to their homeland. They are also in a position to contribute to long-term economic and social development by investing their accumulated capital, transferring skills and facilitating links between their home country and larger foreign markets. Despite the strong attachment, however, many of the diaspora view the financial risk to investments, lack of support, political fragmentation, and weak institutional framework as barriers to investment. As such, they are often caught between isolation and assimilation.

1.6. Outline of the Book

The next two chapters present the theoretical foundations of the analysis and implications. Chapter 2, 'Entrepreneurship, the Diaspora, and Return', sets out the contemporary literature on entrepreneurship and its role in economic development. It then explicitly examines the specific role of returnee entrepreneurship, and the potential impacts of returnee entrepreneurship to home countries. Chapter 3, 'Returnee Entrepreneurship and Institutions', defines institutions and examines how they evolve over time and influence entrepreneurial activity. It then examines how the development of institutions impacts entrepreneurship in different institutional contexts, with a particular focus on post-conflict economies. The chapter contrasts post-conflict economies with other dynamic and changing institutional environments, outlining their distinctiveness in terms of the institutional challenges they face. The chapter then presents the context of the empirical elements of the book, namely B&H, Kosovo, and Montenegro.

Chapters 4 through 8 then present the empirical analysis, drawing on literature reviews, in-depth interviews, and surveys. Chapter 4, 'Bringing the Diaspora Home: Policy Development and Priorities for Returnee Investment', begins by examining the policy approaches being used in B&H, Kosovo, and Montenegro to engage the diaspora, as well as providing implications for other economies. The chapter demonstrates that diaspora engagement is not always a 'win-win' (Pellerin and Mullings, 2013) and there are distinct challenges for policy makers in ensuring that it impacts positively on economic development. The chapter shows that mobilising the diaspora is a central strategic priority for economic development in each post-conflict economies. Yet strategic vision has not translated into policy practice, and as such the potential importance of the diaspora is currently underdeveloped and characterised by a lack of coordination, in part due to ongoing political fragmentation. At the same time, the fact that the connectivity to their homeland of diasporas weakens over time means that there is a pressing need for effective, coordinated policy now. The disparate nature of provision which currently exists means that the mobilisation of diaspora investment is not being maximised. While the flow of remittances, which play a significant role in the economies of the Balkans, demonstrates that diaspora connections are in place, the spillover effect produced by the transfer of knowledge (Riddle and Brinkerhoff, 2011) is not being adequately harnessed.

Chapter 5, 'Intention to Return: The Responses of Returnees to Home Institutional Environments', examines the strategic responses of diaspora entrepreneurs to institutional challenges, utilising a survey of individuals returning to Kosovo. The chapter draws on a survey of the diaspora travelling back to Kosovo, and analyses their intentions to return to live and/or set up a business. The chapter demonstrates that intentions vary among the diaspora, with business experience having a negative relationship on the probability to return, as many will have stable businesses in their host countries and thus the temptation to invest at home will be reduced. The chapter also shows that those with professional and qualified jobs are more likely to have intentions to return, but are less likely to have entrepreneurial intentions. This contrasts with existing research on returnee entrepreneurs to fast-growing economies where international experience can act as an impetus to undertake entrepreneurship at home. In post-conflict economies, international experience acts to temper the potential for entrepreneurial activity at home, reflecting how the knowledge gained is not directly replicable at home due to unstable institutions and different business practices.

Chapter 6, 'How Emotional Ties Influence the Diaspora to Return', examines the role of emotional ties in fostering diaspora entrepreneurs to return and invest in their home country. The chapter utilises in-depth interviews with returnee entrepreneurs to B&H, Kosovo, and Montenegro, and draws on the theory of embeddedness (Jack and Anderson, 2002). A total of 43 in-depth qualitative interviews were conducted, 13 with Bosnian, 21 with Kosovar, and 9 with Montenegrin entrepreneurs. Interviews took place in the capitals of B&H, Kosovo, and Montenegro (Sarajevo, Prishtina, and Podgorica, respectively), as well as in Brussels and Berlin, where networks of the diaspora are present and were interviewees were identified through snowball sampling. The chapter finds that while entrepreneurship is often considered to be a profit-maximising activity (Bylund and McCaffrey, 2017), in the case of returnee entrepreneurs to post-conflict economies, other motivations can be more prevalent. Indeed the analysis demonstrates that for entrepreneurs returning to post-conflict economies, an emotional attachment to the home country is the most important driver of activity. Furthermore, the desire for emotional gains influences investment activities over time, often leading to investment in family and friends, or activities which have a social impact.

Chapter 7, 'The Impact of Internal Displacement and External Migration on Institutional Trust', analyses distinctions between internally displaced and externally displaced entrepreneurs. The chapter draws on a survey of internally displaced and external migrants, as well as in-depth interviews with returnee entrepreneurs, in B&H. Focusing on the complexities of politically and ethnically divided B&H, the chapter demonstrates that internal and external migrants have different levels of trust in home institutions, and that this is related to their exposure to institutional environments abroad. Those migrants who moved abroad are able to compare the home environment to the relative stability they experienced in their host country, meaning that perceptions will be more negative. Internal migrants are more philosophical about the institutional environment, accepting that it is weak and not expecting it to change. At the same time, the chapter shows that individuals with more diverse ethnic networks, caused either by exposure to different groups abroad or by moving into and/or working with different groups at home, will have lower trust in institutions. This can be explained by institutions not being ethnically neutral and individuals being exposed to discrimination, either directly themselves or through the experiences of others in their network.

Chapter 8, 'Engaging Returnee Entrepreneurs Through Institutional Change', returns the analysis to policy making and institution building. Through in-depth interviews with policy makers and other stakeholders in B&H, Kosovo, and Montenegro, the chapter investigates perceptions of, and progress towards, engaging returnee entrepreneurs. It demonstrates that while policy makers are aware of the importance of emotional ties to home, they have little influence over it and instead need to focus on the practicalities of improving the institutional environment. The chapter shows that policy emphasis has been placed on formal institutional reform, in particular the regulative framework, rather than ideational politics which emphasises heritage and cultural promotion (Waldinger, 2015). Yet in all three countries reforms have been slow. This serves to discourage growing investment from the diaspora, as risks are often considered to be too great. Positive reforms are required so that the second generation of migrants do not become more isolated from their parents' homeland. If that connection is lost, investments will only decrease over time.

Chapter 9, 'Conclusions: Implications for Theory, Policy, and Practice', closes the book with a comparative analysis of the key theoretical frameworks employed in the book in order to illuminate the contribution of returnee entrepreneurs to complex environments. The chapter articulates the specific components of isolation and assimilation, detailing that while individuals are returning to complex homelands, their contributions are not currently being maximised. They are not assimilated within the economy, often avoiding policy actions designed to engage with them. This will have a lasting impact on the potential of returnees to contribute to their homeland, especially given that the emotional ties of the first generation are stronger than subsequent generations, and thus interest in homeland return may diminish over time.

2

Entrepreneurship, the Diaspora, and Return

2.1. Introduction

This chapter sets out the importance of entrepreneurship in economic development. It then builds on this by reviewing the contemporary literature related to returnee entrepreneurship. The chapter highlights the resurgent interest in entrepreneurship among economic theorists and the increased importance ascribed to entrepreneurship by policy makers. It also demonstrates that often research focuses on entrepreneurs within a country, region, or locality, rather than entrepreneurs who are global actors moving across international borders. Of the research on flows of entrepreneurs outside national borders, the majority of literature focuses on the impacts in host countries (i.e. the country they have emigrated to), rather than their home country (i.e. the country they have emigrated from). For example, Ram et al. (2008) examine Somali entrepreneurs and Vershinina et al. (2011) examine Polish entrepreneurs in the United Kingdom; Baycan-Levent and Nijkamp (2009) investigate migrant entrepreneurship in eight European countries, while Wang and Liu (2015) and Lassmann and Busch (2015) examine immigrant entrepreneurial activity among different ethnic groups in the United States. There is some existing research which examines impacts in both home and host countries (see, for example, Patel and Conklin, 2009), and an emerging literature on their home country (see, for example, Gillespie et al., 1999; Nielsen and Riddle, 2010; Riddle et al., 2010; Li et al., 2012; Brinkerhoff, 2016). This chapter develops the key theoretical contributions of the book in examining the potential role that returnee entrepreneurs can play in economic development when they return and invest in their homeland.

2.2. Understanding Entrepreneurship and Economic Development

Entrepreneurship is recognised as a crucial element in fostering economic development and growth (Acs et al., 2008). Romer (2007, p. 128) emphasises

The Diaspora and Returnee Entrepreneurship. Nick Williams, Oxford University Press (2021). © Oxford University Press.
DOI: 10.1093/oso/9780190911874.003.0002

the role of entrepreneurship by stating that 'economic growth occurs whenever people take resources and rearrange them in ways that are valuable. . . . [It] springs from better recipes, not just more cooking'. The process of entrepreneurship is widely considered to stimulate competition, drive innovation, create employment, generate positive externalities, increase productivity by introducing technological change, and provide a route out of poverty (Acs, 2006).

Across major industrialised economies, levels of entrepreneurial activity are positively correlated with levels of per capita gross domestic product (GDP) and the rate of GDP growth (Acs, 2006; Huggins and Williams, 2009). Additionally, entrepreneurship is playing a key role in emerging economies (Bruton et al., 2010). As a result, around the world government intervention within the field of entrepreneurship is inspired by the view that the entrepreneur is one of the solutions to weak economic performance and poor levels of job creation (Holtz-Eakin, 2000; Audretsch et al., 2007).

In the past, the prevailing view of economists was that large-scale enterprises were the key to economic development, while small firms were viewed as relatively inefficient and less involved in innovative activity (Audretsch et al., 2006). The notion that economic growth was possible without the innovations of individual entrepreneurs gained support (Galbraith, 1956; Chandler, 1977), with small firms and entrepreneurship viewed as a luxury rather than a necessity (Audretsch et al., 2006). The route to economic growth was seen as being a combination of large-scale production and collectivist ideologies, and stability, continuity, and homogeneity became the cornerstones of 'managed' economies (Verheul et al., 2001). However, the domination of 'big-firm capitalism' has gradually diminished (Storey, 1994), and the role and importance of the entrepreneur has witnessed a resurgence in both economic theory and public policy (Audretsch, 2003).

In the past, entrepreneurship policies were often developed as a temporary solution to absorb workers displaced by industrial restructuring and downsizing (Storey, 1991). Yet in more recent years such policies are seen as an essential instrument for encouraging economic growth (Gilbert et al., 2004). However, the notion of the entrepreneur and the contribution of entrepreneurship to economic growth have been widely interpreted (Hébert and Link, 1989), and as such there exists no generally accepted definition. Sautet and Kirzner (2006) argue that the concept of entrepreneurship is notoriously difficult to pin down, with economists and policy makers often entirely overlooking it or gravely misunderstanding it. This chapter illuminates the debates regarding the role of the entrepreneur and the centrality of entrepreneurship to economic growth.

2.2.1. The Role of the Entrepreneur

Over time, entrepreneurship has been used to define types of individuals (Say, 2006), types of decisions (Knight, 1921), and forms of behaviour (Schumpeter, 1934). As a discrete concept, entrepreneurship has its origin in the work of Cantillon (1931) and has developed through the neoclassical school's emphasis on equilibrium. The neoclassical model, which links stocks of capital and labour to growth, dominated growth theory (Solow, 1956; Audretsch, 2007). However, entrepreneurship did not fit into this model as the neoclassical axiom of perfect competition implies that there are no profit opportunities for entrepreneurs left to exploit, and, secondly, models of general equilibrium do not take into account the dynamics of innovating entrepreneurship (Wennekers and Thurik, 1999). This has led to theoretical challenges based on the notion that entrepreneurship is crucial to understanding economic growth (Kirzner, 1979).

The entrepreneur plays a central role in market process theory. As Kirzner (1973) states '[t]he market process is always entrepreneurial, and the entrepreneurial process is always competitive' (pp. 102–103). The competitive process of the market consists of a series of competitive discoveries, and as such is a rivalrous discovery process (Sautet and Kirzner, 2006). It is argued that the 'perfect competition' of the equilibrium model is incompatible with the idea of real market competition (Douhan et al., 2007). Market process theory posits that the entrepreneur exploits previously unnoticed profit opportunities, which do not exist in the 'perfect competition' model (Kirzner, 1973, 1982; Douhan et al., 2007). Where there are unexploited profit opportunities, the theory states that resources have been misallocated and that entrepreneurship corrects this waste (Kirzner, 1982). These opportunities were 'utterly unknown' and 'not known to be knowable' which is the underlying basis of the neoclassical model (Douhan et al., 2007). By exploiting these opportunities and discovering more efficient ways of utilising resources, the entrepreneurial process shifts the entire production possibility curve. This shift represents the essence of economic growth, causing an increase in real output due to increases in real productivity (Kirzner, 1985).

The actions of co-operating individuals trigger the market process. The market is in constant disequilibrium, continuously adjusting, generating, and transmitting information, and providing incentives for action and exchange (Kirzner, 1973). The desire to make profit stimulates the entrepreneurs to employ the most efficient use of resources, and entrepreneurs introduce innovation in order to adjust to consumer desires. Buyers and sellers seek information in order to participate in the market, and although information is subjective and limited (Hayek, 1945), economic actors need only a little information in order to act on their expectations of the future (Kirzner, 1973; Shane, 2000; Boettke and Coyne, 2003). This means that entrepreneurs can act on opportunities based on their own idiosyncratic experience and knowledge (Shane, 2000).

Human action is required for entrepreneurship to take place, with boldness, imagination, and creativity as important aspects in this action (Schumpeter, 1942; Kirzner, 1973, 2009). As a key exponent of the importance of entrepreneurship, Schumpeter states that innovation is at its core. The entrepreneur creates new circumstances which cause disequilibrium and leads to 'gales of creative destruction', in which old methods of production and organisation were destroyed and replaced by the new forms (Schumpeter, 1942). In Schumpeter's analysis, the factory wiped out the blacksmith shop, the car took over the horse and carriage, and the corporation overthrew the proprietorship (McCraw, 2007). To Schumpeter, the entrepreneur is a leader, and therefore contrasted with the many 'imitators' who follow the innovative lead of entrepreneurs (Kirzner, 1999; Schumpeter, 1942). Moreover, the Schumpeterian entrepreneur is a heroic figure motivated by 'the dream and will to create a private kingdom', with the 'will to conquer; the impulse to fight, to prove oneself superior to others, to succeed for the sake, not of the fruits of success, but of success itself' (Schumpeter, 1934, pp. 93–94). By doing so, Schumpeter's entrepreneur drives an economy forward by creating new production possibilities (Schumpeter, 1934, 1942; Westlund and Bolton, 2003).

In contrast, Kirzner (1973) states that entrepreneurship does not necessarily require innovation. While the Schumpeterian entrepreneur causes dramatic changes in markets and industries, the Kirznerian entrepreneur engages in arbitrage by being alert to profit opportunities in existing circumstances (Kirzner, 1973, 2009). In this sense, entrepreneurship does not necessarily require originality or innovation; more simply, it requires alertness to opportunity. By discovering opportunities, the entrepreneur moves the economy towards equilibrium rather than by a disequilibrating force (see Table 2.1 for a summary of these theoretical differences).

Despite these different theoretical interpretations, it is clear that entrepreneurship involves the nexus of entrepreneurial opportunities and enterprising individuals, with the ability to identify opportunities being a key part of the entrepreneurial process (Shane, 2003). This means that entrepreneurship is not only concerned with the launch of new ventures. While the creation of a new business is an accurate description of one of the many outcomes of entrepreneurial activity, entrepreneurship encompasses far

Table 2.1 Schumpeterian Opportunities versus Kirznerian Opportunities

Schumpeterian Opportunities	Kirznerian Opportunities
Disequilibrating	Equilibrating
Requires new information	Does not require new information
Very innovative	Less innovative
Rare	Common
Involves creation	Limited to discovery

Source: Shane (2003, Box 2.1).

more than business start-ups, and derives from the creative power of the human mind (Sautet and Kirzner, 2006), characterised as a behavioural characteristic of individuals expressed through innovative attributes, flexibility, and/or adaptability to change (Swedberg, 2000; Wennekers and Thurik, 1999).

Economic theory holds explicit implications for government intervention to promote entrepreneurship. Both Schumpeterian and Kirznerian views are important in terms of policy intervention, since if government can influence levels and types of entrepreneurship it is a lever by which to harness economic development. Building on this, Baumol (1990) proposes that the supply of entrepreneurship is constant, but its distribution across productive, unproductive, and destructive activities is affected by institutional arrangements and the social pay-off structure.

Baumol's (1990) theory implies that government action has the possibility of promoting all three activities. A key issue is that policy may promote unproductive activities through incentivised 'rent seeking' based on acquiring government grants, resulting in entrepreneurs moving away from previously productive activities that satisfied consumer desires and led to economic growth. Nevertheless, policies geared towards enhancing entrepreneurship and stimulating enterprise development have become increasingly prevalent across advanced economies (Gilbert et al., 2004). Reflecting the raised importance of entrepreneurship over the last two decades, economic development policies have shifted away from trying to attract large manufacturing firms and inward investment towards fostering entrepreneurship (Sobel et al., 2007). In environments which allow free entry into the market, entrepreneurs can take advantage of new profit opportunities and create new entrepreneurial possibilities that others can act upon (Minniti, 2005). As such, entrepreneurship creates an environment that makes even more entrepreneurship possible (Holcombe, 2007).

2.2.2. Motivations of Entrepreneurs

In addition to debates regarding definitions and the role of enterprise in society, the motivations of entrepreneurs are the subject of debate (Smallbone and Welter, 2004; Shane, 2009). Analysing the entrepreneurship literature over the past few decades, numerous taxonomies have been developed to order the competing motivations for undertaking entrepreneurial activity. In recent years, a particular classificatory schema has become increasingly pervasive. Despite the well-rehearsed earlier assertions that the complex and diverse motives of entrepreneurs must not be oversimplified by simplistic explanatory models, a large and ever growing stream of thought has nevertheless adopted a basic dichotomous depiction of entrepreneurs as either necessity-driven, pushed into entrepreneurship because all other options for work are absent or unsatisfactory, or opportunity-driven, pulled into entrepreneurial activity out of choice to exploit business opportunity (Hechaverria and Reynolds, 2009; Nikolaev et al., 2018).

This dichotomous classification has moved ever more centre stage in the contemporary entrepreneurship literature, with one prominent reason being its usage in the Global Entrepreneurship Monitor (GEM), the predominant global survey of the degree and nature of entrepreneurship which covers 35 countries (Global Entrepreneurship Monitor, 2018). GEM aims to explore the link between entrepreneurship and economic development within and across countries, and in doing so makes a distinction between 'necessity entrepreneurship' and 'opportunity entrepreneurship'. Similar to much of the literature that adopts this binary depiction of entrepreneurship, nevertheless, GEM treats necessity- and opportunity-driven entrepreneurs as entirely separate categories. As Minniti et al. (2006, p. 21) assert in relation to the GEM survey, 'In most countries . . . nearly all individuals can be sorted into one of the two categories'. In GEM, in consequence, the a priori assumption is that necessity- and opportunity-driven entrepreneurship are constituted via their negation to each other (i.e. to be an entrepreneur out of choice means that one is not doing so out of necessity).

While Lazear (2005, p. 650) adopts an old adage when he states that 'as necessity is the mother of invention, perhaps entrepreneurs are created when a worker has no alternatives', a growing number of studies have begun to question not only the separateness of opportunity and necessity and whether they might coexist in entrepreneurs' motives, but also the temporal fluidity of motivations. One issue, however, has been that much of the literature calling for this dualistic depiction to be transcended has focused on what might be deemed entrepreneurship in the 'margins' rather than mainstream entrepreneurship. Studies have focused, on the one hand, on entrepreneurship in transition economies such as East-Central Europe (Aidis et al., 2008; Smallbone and Welter, 2004), and on the other hand, on entrepreneurs operating in the off-the-books economy (Gurtoo and Williams, 2009). Nevertheless, it is becoming increasingly recognised that entrepreneurial motivations are complex, with the opportunity/necessity dualism being overly simplistic. Indeed, there have been calls to transcend this representation and recognise that entrepreneurs move through various motivations through the pre-launch, start-up, and growth phases of entrepreneurial activity (Williams and Williams, 2012).

As well as the dualism of opportunity versus necessity entrepreneurship, a further common depiction of entrepreneurial motivations is the pursuit of profit. Entrepreneurship is often viewed as entry into business activities that rely on market exchange structures, with the individual's objective being to maximise profits. While it would be foolish to deny that entrepreneurship can often be defined as the exploitation of opportunities for monetary profit, and that this can drive forward innovation, the pursuit of profits may not always be the priority (Benz, 2005, 2009). Instead, many may engage in activity for social reasons (Benz, 2009). Social entrepreneurs are often defined as seeking to address societal rather than commercial needs, through social wealth creation (Zahra et al., 2009). In this sense, social entrepreneurs can be conceptualised as generating positive externalities, with the value created by the enterprise accruing to wider society and which will not be contained within the market exchange in which the enterprise is engaged (Santos, 2012). This is contrasted with commercial entrepreneurs who may also generate positive externalities, for example through job creation, but is seen as a side effect of activity rather than an objective (Estrin et al., 2016).

As with the dichotomy of opportunity and necessity entrepreneurship, the division of profit and social entrepreneurs is also problematic. Often, entrepreneurs do not pursue either purely commercial or social goals. Instead, many can have profit and social motivations when describing their entrepreneurial endeavours (Williams and Williams, 2012). At the same time, motivations do not remain static. As such, entrepreneurs can move through commercial to social motivations and back again.

2.2.3. Entrepreneurship and Place

Debates regarding the motivations of entrepreneurs demonstrate the role of place in determining entrepreneurial activity. Place influences the motivations of entrepreneurs as well as the returns that can be made through activity. As Chapter 1 made clear, context, i.e. the place in which activity is undertaken, matters for entrepreneurship.

In examining place, a key aspect of theory is the notion of knowledge spillovers. Knowledge is often considered to be a public good that frequently 'spills over' to other firms and individuals, allowing others to reap what they have not necessarily sown (Acs et al., 2009), Knowledge spillovers can be defined as the continuum between pure knowledge spillovers that are uncharged, unintended, and not mediated by any market mechanism, and rent spillovers consisting of externalities that are at least partially paid for (Andersson and Ejermo, 2005). While endogenous growth theory assumes that the spillover process is automatic, it is in fact a process driven by economic agents, i.e. entrepreneurs (Audretsch and Keilbach, 2004). Entrepreneurs convert freely available knowledge into economic knowledge (Braunerhjelm et al., 2009) and by doing so they guide the market, driving the selection process, creating a diversity of knowledge, and fostering the market process (Sautet and Kirzner, 2006). The start-up of new firms contributes to diversity by commercialising knowledge (Acs and Plummer, 2005); the greater the level of entrepreneurship, the greater the diversity and resultant growth (Audretsch and Keilbach, 2004).

Knowledge spillovers may occur through the flow of skills, expertise, technology, R&D, and the like across inter-organisational and interpersonal networks (Andersson and Karlsson, 2007). The spillover effects of knowledge can take place through time and across space, with the general argument being that knowledge spills over more easily locally than at a distance. Entrepreneurs and firms benefit from local knowledge spillovers as an undirected and spontaneous 'buzz'; they may also need to consciously build non-local 'pipelines' to tap into knowledge from outside (Bathelt et al., 2004). Knowledge spillovers will not be uniform across all firms and places. The study of entrepreneurship has increasingly reflected the general agreement that entrepreneurs and new firms must engage in networks to survive (Anderson et al., 2010). Also, it is accepted that the socio-economic climate in which entrepreneurs operate will vary their ability to capture the benefits of economic efficiency that networks facilitate (Jack, 2005; Bowey and Easton, 2007). Research on the networking behaviour of entrepreneurs has tended to focus on personal-social and professional networks as contributing to the success potential of a venture (Aldrich and Zimmer, 1986). Entrepreneurship models of networking have mainly incorporated social-network and resource-dependence theories, as well as a resource-based view of the entrepreneur (Ostgaard and Birley, 1996). Network perspectives are seen as contributing to explaining patterns of entrepreneurship, by which it is the social role and embedded social context that facilitates or inhibits the activities of entrepreneurs (Aldrich and Zimmer, 1986). Networks matter to entrepreneurs because they create efficiencies in assembling the resources necessary in the entrepreneurial process.

Where knowledge spillovers are effective and utilised, they can contribute to enabling more positive cultures of entrepreneurship. Culture lies at the core of entrepreneurship conceptualised as a set of shared values, beliefs, and expected behaviours (Hayton et al., 2002; Huggins and Williams, 2011). Culture shapes what individuals perceive as opportunities, and therefore entrepreneurial alertness is linked to judgment, creativity, and interpretation (Hofstede, 1991; Sautet and Kirzner, 2006). Effective institutions[1] and a culture supportive of entrepreneurship make it possible for economic actors to take advantage of perceived opportunities (Sautet and Kirzner, 2006). Places (countries, regions, cities, or smaller communities) with an entrepreneurially-conducive culture may increase their competitive advantage by attracting investment, skills, and talent (Turok, 2004). Those places with strong entrepreneurial traditions have a competitive advantage if they are able to perpetuate it over time and generations (Audretsch and Fritsch, 2002; Parker, 2004; Mueller, 2006). Entrepreneurship capital, referring to the capacity of a society to generate entrepreneurial activity, is built up and has a positive impact on economic performance (Audretsch and Keilbach, 2005). In contrast, those places lacking a history of entrepreneurship will struggle to foster effective cultures (Williams and Vorley, 2015).

Entrepreneurship can be considered to be self-reinforcing in nature and can concentrate geographically because of the social environment, as individuals follow societal clues and are influenced by what others have chosen to do (Feldman, 2001; Minniti, 2005). Entrepreneurial activity creates its own feedback cycle, slowly moving society to a more entrepreneurial culture, with a high density of successful new venture creation by local entrepreneurs offering role models people can conform to (Verheul et al., 2001). Places, therefore, can influence entrepreneurial activities via a shared culture or set of formal and informal rules (Werker and Athreye, 2004). In places where entrepreneurship is seen as providing valuable rewards, and entrepreneurs are seen as role models, a sustaining entrepreneurial culture can be formed (Saxenian, 1996). However, changes in levels of entrepreneurship and contributions to economic development will take time to emerge, and as such any impacts may only be seen in the long term (Huggins and Williams, 2009).

---

[1] For more on the role of institutions, see Chapter 3.

A key cultural trait of places is their social capital, consisting of the economic significance of social relations facilitated through personal contacts, networks, and norms of behaviour (Granovetter, 1973; Coleman, 1990, 2000; Westlund and Bolton, 2003; Liao and Welsch, 2005). Spatial approaches to entrepreneurship and economic development are often built on theories of social capital (Putnam, 1995), which can be defined as 'the ability of individuals to secure benefits as a result of membership in social networks or other social structures' (World Bank, 2000, p. 128). In this sense, social capital is linked to, but distinct from, human capital, which can be defined as individual-related resources (Becker, 1996; Lee and Jones, 2008).

As Adler and Kwon (2002) state, in tight-knit communities strong norms may dictate the sharing of resources among extended family members, which may, in turn, reduce the incentives for entrepreneurial activity and slow the accumulation of capital. However, individual actors in a social setting cannot be wholly calculating and opportunistic as no-one would trade with them; yet neither can they be entirely reciprocating and trusting as they may open themselves up to exploitation (Axelrod, 1985; Seabright, 2004).

To illustrate how social capital operates positively, Coleman (2000) uses the example of the diamond market in New York to illustrate the fact that pre-existing social relations enable economic actors to achieve outcomes which would otherwise be unobtainable. While negotiating a sale, diamond traders routinely give other merchants a bag of valuable diamonds to examine in private without any formal guarantee that the buyers will not replace any of the stones in an effort to get a better deal. The arrangement benefits the smooth functioning operation of the diamond wholesale market, and is only possible because merchants belong to 'essentially a closed community', sharing ethnic, religious, family, and community ties (Coleman, 2000, p. 17). As is clear in Coleman's example, networks and trust are important aspects of social capital within a community.

2.2.4. Embeddedness and Entrepreneurial Activity

An important element in understanding context and place of entrepreneurship is embeddedness. Embeddedness is the nature, depth, and extent of an individual's ties into the environment (Dacin et al., 1999; Jack and Anderson, 2002). The theory of embeddedness emphasises the fact that entrepreneurship is a socialised process (Drakopolou Dodd and Anderson, 2007), and as such there is a relationship between the entrepreneurial self and society (Jack and Anderson, 2002; Uzzi, 1997). Embeddedness explains how context and community influence perceived possibilities in particular situations (Welter, 2011) and acts to either enable or constrain entrepreneurial activity (Johnstone and Lionais, 2004). Embeddedness describes how change is not driven by purely economically rational individuals with stable preference functions, but instead recognises different and changing social norms and values (McKeever et al., 2015).

By being embedded, the entrepreneur becomes part of the social context through systems of social relations, networks, bonds, and local ties (Granovetter, 1985; Kalantaridis and Bika, 2006). It is within and through these persistent social structures that entrepreneurs can create and extract value from their environments (Hansen, 1995). Portes and Sensenbrenner (1993) explained that embeddedness is an important mechanism for identifying opportunities and for understanding the protocols through which resources are distributed, shared, and put to use. Embeddedness provides and connects shared values, within-group trust, historical reciprocity, and bounded solidarity, which are privileged aspects of local belonging (Anderson et al., 2012).

Embeddedness thus emphasises the importance of the social in shaping entrepreneurial practices. By focusing on situated roles and relationships, and how these influence action, a more holistic and situated view of entrepreneurship can be generated (McKeever et al., 2015). It is important to distinguish between structural and relational embeddedness (Granovetter, 1992). Structural embeddedness is concerned with the impersonal configuration of linkages between people or units, whereas relational embeddedness relates to the individuals' personal relationships with other individuals such as family members or friends (Bird and Wennberg, 2016). Previous research has shown that this element is critical in supporting immigrants' economic endeavours (Granovetter, 1992). The majority of studies focus on entrepreneurs within a country (Jack and Anderson, 2002; McKeever et al., 2015). There are studies of internationalisation and embeddedness at the organisational/sectoral level; for example, Meuleman et al. (2017) focus on relation embeddedness of cross-border venture capital; and Al-Laham and Souitaris (2008) examine network embeddedness and internationalisation of German biotech industries. Furthermore, studies of immigration such as Kalantaridis and Bika (2006) and Bird and Wennberg (2016) have examined different forms of in-migrant embeddedness, and Lin et al. (2018) utilise embeddedness theory but focus on the maintenance of networks at home while the individual is overseas. Yet understanding the value of embeddedness in relation to returnee entrepreneurs is currently under-researched, and especially as related to complex institutional environments.

2.3. Returnee Entrepreneurship

The preceding section demonstrated the important role that entrepreneurial activity plays in economic development. This section sets out the role that returnee entrepreneurship can play in economic development. Returnee entrepreneurs are defined as individuals who have moved away from their home country and have lived and/or worked in a host country, and then have later returned to their home country to live, invest, or both (Filatotchev et al., 2009; Lin et al., 2018).

Extant research on return migration provides mixed results, from the positive impact of Silicon Valley entrepreneurs connecting their homeland to California and the impact of return to rural China, to less positive and mixed results in Europe, for example in Albania and Southern Italy (Hausmann and Nedelkoska, 2018). The results are positive in studies of high-tech diaspora entrepreneurs, who can connect their homelands to clusters of activity such as Silicon Valley (Saxenian, 1999). In most cases, as Hausmann and Nedelkoska (2018) state, the outcomes depend on whether returnees engage in self-employment or employment, with self-employment often the choice of those who have gained relevant skills and experience in the host country.

One group which has received attention in the research are the 'sea turtles' returning to China. Lin et al. (2018) state that over the past 10 years returnees to China have increased markedly, with 5,237,000 students going abroad and 409,100 returning in 2015, a reflux ration of 78% compared to 30% in 2005. Such returnees are viewed as strategically important to a growing economy like China due to their contribution to upgrading skills and technology in the home country (Qin et al., 2017). Desirable returnee entrepreneurs are viewed as those individuals who can bring back advanced technology in scarce supply in the home country (Williams, 2018). Yet even given their importance, and policy attention focused on harnessing return, such individuals face many barriers: labour and land costs are rising, protection of intellectual property rights is still problematic, and corruption is widespread (The Economist, 2013).

2.3.1. The Diaspora and Return

With increasing movements of people around the world, the majority of countries now have established diaspora communities living and working abroad. The diaspora are dispersed ethnic and national groups across international borders who also maintain a relationship to their home country (Safran,

1991). These relationships can be harnessed to benefit their home country in a number of ways: through the sharing of capital (Mullings, 2011), technical knowledge (Oettl and Agrawal, 2008), expectations of how business should be conducted (Riddle and Brinkerhoff, 2011), direct investment (Turnock, 2001), and the harnessing of entrepreneurial activity (Williams, 2018). This entrepreneurial activity can be fostered by the diaspora in their home countries in three key ways: first, by direct involvement in the creation of new firms or the management of existing firms; second, by investing in the entrepreneurial activities of others; and, third, by acting as a role model and inspiration to entrepreneurs in the home country (Mayer et al., 2015). The role model 'demonstration effect', whereby residents in the diaspora's country of origin are encouraged into economic activity as a result of the increased investment from abroad, can be significant in countries with low levels of entrepreneurship (Riddle et al., 2010).

The diaspora can serve as a vital bridge between their host countries and home countries, promoting and facilitating economic and political ties (Brinkerhoff, 2016), and utilising formal and informal networks (Levin and Barnard, 2013). First-generation diaspora members are likely to have strong informal network ties to their home country because of relationships established before emigrating, and more formal networks are built over time through business experience and success (Mayer et al., 2015). While diaspora networks vary in terms of the number of actors they incorporate, their location, the benefits they provide to individual members, and the strength of relations between network actors can all influence economic activity (Li et al., 2017). Within the home country, diaspora networks can allow access to resources that are unavailable or more expensive to acquire from other sources, and provide access to new markets for goods and services (Smallbone et al., 2010). Migrants who operate abroad often gain knowledge and skills that are lacking in the home country (Nielsen and Riddle, 2010). When they return to invest or start a new business, they remit this acquired human capital back to the home country, thereby turning 'brain drain' into 'brain gain' (Stark, 2004).

While the economic impacts of transnational diaspora entrepreneurship are highly significant, the non-economic impacts have been described as at least as significant to the social, cultural, and political environments in the home country (Kshetri, 2013). This not only can benefit individual family and friends with whom the diaspora have contacts, but can also bring about institutional changes (i.e. changes to the rules which govern entrepreneurial activity) through the influence of policy makers (Riddle and Brinkerhoff, 2011). As such, economies which can mobilise and harness the assets of the diaspora community can accelerate economic development.

Diaspora communities maintain a relationship to their country of origin (Nielsen and Riddle, 2010; Riddle and Brinkerhoff, 2011), and this (often emotional) tie means that the diaspora often adopt transnational characteristics which are a mix of learned cultural and social behaviours from their country of origin and host country (Kshetri, 2013). Economies aiming to attract investment from their emigrant diaspora communities, often referred to as diaspora direct investment (DDI) (see, for example, Newland and Tanaka, 2010), are often less economically developed. Any increase in DDI has a significant positive effect on economic development, and also has a wider impact of influencing perceptions of the investment climate, which can in turn lead to an increase in national investment (Gillespie et al., 1999). Furthermore, DDI triggers a 'demonstration effect', whereby residents in the diaspora's country of origin are encouraged into economic activity as a result of the increased investment from abroad (Riddle et al., 2010).

2.3.2. The Diaspora and the Liability of Foreignness

While living in the host country, the diaspora have not been exposed to the domestic environment, which can be fast changing and unstable (Qin et al., 2017). When returning, an understanding of the local context is important due to distinct regulatory environments (Leblang, 2010; Zhou, 2013). Understanding the local environment takes time, and unfamiliarity may constitute a large obstacle to return (Qin et al., 2017). As such, returnees may face a 'liability of foreignness', meaning that they face social and economic costs when operating in foreign markets (Johanson and Vahlne, 2009).

Entrepreneurs seeking to internationalise need to build relationship-specific social capital to overcome this liability (Johanson and Vahlne, 2009). Because trust builds slowly, especially with non-domestic entities who might have little reputation within the target market, the process of international expansion can be slow and gradual (Autio, 2017). However, if networks at home have been maintained, then returnee entrepreneurs may be able to overcome this liability (Zaheer, 1995). Informal networks of family and friends can support activity, filling gaps in local knowledge for the returnee. In this way, returnees can overcome the liability by becoming (re)connected with local constituents and developing an understanding of social, cultural, and institutional changes at home (Li et al., 2012). Such 'relational' embeddedness allows intangible resources, such as information, support, and know-how, and tangible resources, such as financial loans, to be accessed (Moran, 2005). As such, it represents a property derived from the individual's relationships with others, and can often be gained through family members (Bird and Wennberg, 2016).

Overcoming this liability may have an impact on the entry modes used by returnee entrepreneurs and also may influence the strategic decisions made in the development of their activities. The effective utilisation of networks is important, as returnee entrepreneurs are likely to have strong informal network ties to their home country that result from relationships established before migration (Brinkerhoff, 2016). More formal networks are then built over time in the home country through business experience. Networks provide benefits to individual entrepreneurs, and the strength of relationships between network actors will influence activity (Li et al., 2017). This means that accessing networks may be critical in overcoming the liability of foreignness. It also demonstrates that internationalisation is not necessarily a process of accumulating 'foreign market knowledge'; rather, it is a process of expanding network relationships abroad (Autio, 2017). Thus embeddedness is important as it is precisely through engagement with friends and family that returnee entrepreneurs may act.

2.3.3. Engaging with the Diaspora: Remittances and Beyond

The diaspora have long been courted by their home countries for financial remittances (Klekowski von Koppenfels, 2017; Gamlen et al., 2017), and these can make a significant contribution to the home economy (Vaaler, 2013; Martinez et al., 2015). Remittances commonly go towards supporting friends and family and are an example of the diaspora communities' sense of moral responsibility to benefit the development of their home country, created by their emotional ties and connections. Zheng and Musteen (2018) find that remittances can lead to new business venturing driven by necessity, i.e. when individuals turn to entrepreneurship due to lack of other employment opportunities; yet it may lead to decreased levels of opportunity entrepreneurship. This, they state, is because necessity entrepreneurship generally requires relatively low levels of financial and human capital and little opportunity costs from the viewpoint of the entrepreneur (Thurik et al., 2008). In contrast, opportunity entrepreneurship involves higher risks given its longer payoff horizon and novel business model. Vaaler (2011) found that remittances are positively associated with new venture creation rates, but only in countries where the state does not 'crowd out' private players, because that state policy may encourage accumulation of venture funds to create fewer but larger enterprises and focus on opportunity-driven entrepreneurship. In addition, Martinez et al. (2015) find that remittances are most effective as a venture funding source in countries with substantial informal sectors. While these studies are important in understanding financial flows from the diaspora, research has moved beyond consideration of remittances as the key source of transfer from those living outside the country (Clemens et al., 2014). Indeed, the role of remittances has been called into question, with Brinkerhoff (2016) stating that they are primarily household transfers, providing income that is often essential to sustenance but that could be applied for a variety of purposes, including conspicuous consumption.[2]

Beyond remittances, the diaspora can contribute to their country of origin through the transfer of knowledge (Riddle et al., 2010). This works thorough both social and business channels as the diaspora interact with others transnationally and pick up and share skills and ideas. While the economic impacts of transnational diaspora entrepreneurship are highly significant, the non-economic impacts have been described as at least as significant to the social, cultural, and political environments in the country of origin (Kshetri, 2013). This can benefit individual family and friends with whom the diaspora have contacts, but can also bring about institutional changes (i.e. changes to the rules which govern entrepreneurial activity) through the influence of policy makers (Riddle and Brinkerhoff, 2011). As such, economies which can mobilise and harness the assets of the diaspora community can accelerate economic development. Despite this, however, much policy focus has centred on 'extracting obligations' from the diaspora, asking 'what the diaspora can do for them', rather than what they can do for diaspora investors (Gamlen, 2006). In addition, diaspora-specific policies are particularly challenging in post-conflict economies, where government emphasis is on building nascent and fragile institutional environments, and where coordination between different departments and levels of government is often lacking (Nielsen and Riddle, 2010). As diaspora engagement in the homeland can be multidimensional, driven by individuals or through families, through formal and informal networks, their mobilisation can assume different forms of financial and human capital, including remittances, direct investment, philanthropy, and tourism (Nkongolo-Bakenda and Chrysostome, 2013). Given that engagement is multidimensional, policies aimed at mobilising the diaspora are also multidimensional, seeking, for example, to secure remittances, direct investment, and sharing of human and social capital.

---

[2] Chapter 4 discusses further how policy has moved away from remittances as the key focus of engagement with the diaspora.

Diaspora communities can play a very important role in the development of their countries of origin through contributions of various forms and shapes (Faist, 2008; Gamlen, 2014). By sending remittances, diaspora communities improve macroeconomic stability, reduce poverty rates by enabling their family members to meet consumption needs and facilitate human capital formation by enabling higher expenditure on education and health, as well as supporting entrepreneurial activity (Gillespie et al., 1999; Vaaler, 2013). Also, by working and undertaking education in their host countries, diaspora communities accumulate human, financial, and social capital that can be invested for productive purposes in their countries of origin, or gain valuable skills that could be transferred home, where such valuable capitals are often underdeveloped (Riddle and Brinkerhoff, 2011). Furthermore, active diaspora communities can serve as a vital bridge between their host countries and countries of origin, promoting and facilitating economic and political ties (Levin and Barnard, 2013).

Diasporas often take on transnational characteristics, consisting of traits adopted in both their home and host country. These characteristics are often multipolar rather than bipolar, as actors relate to multiple localities, which gives them a unique advantage in conducting transnational business (Bagwell, 2015). Furthermore, diaspora communities often maintain an altruistic tie to their homeland which makes them an ideal target for policy makers, as they are seen as more likely to wish to contribute to their country of origin (Nielsen and Riddle, 2010). In order to contribute, diaspora entrepreneurs utilise their formal and informal networks between their country of origin and host country (Levin and Barnard, 2013). These allow for transfer of knowledge and facilitate trade between countries, as well as offering support and motivation (Gillespie et al., 1999; Vaaler, 2013). Mayer et al. (2015) find that first-generation diaspora members are likely to have strong informal network ties to their country of origin, as they had relationships with native family and friends before emigrating, and that more formal networks are built over time through business experience and success. These networks have been shown to reduce 'space' between countries and so facilitate international trade and commerce as they are able to overcome informal barriers (Kshetri, 2013). While diaspora networks vary in terms of the number of actors they incorporate, their location, the benefits they provide to individual members, and the strength of relations between network actors—all of which can influence economic activity (Smallbone et al., 2010)—these transnational characteristics allow members of diaspora communities to operate in intermediary roles between countries, as they possess the advantage of deeper understanding of social and business environments internationally (Riddle et al., 2008). This assists them not only to develop their own ventures, but also to influence the entrepreneurial activity of others. Indeed, within the country of origin, business owners can exploit diaspora networks in two key ways: first, to access resources that are unavailable or more expensive to acquire from other sources; and second, to provide access to markets for goods and services (Smallbone et al., 2010).

The benefits accrued through these characteristics and networks can be tangible and intangible. Tangible benefits take the form of capital gains, such as financial and human capital, along with improved attractiveness and stimulus for DDI (Ojo et al., 2013; Mayer et al., 2015). Intangible benefits are less easily measured than tangible benefits as they do not hold quantifiable characteristics; however, they can include institutional changes brought about by diaspora activity enhancing the globalisation of business and politics, as well as the transfer of knowledge, which can have a direct impact on entrepreneurial activity or can act as inspiration to home-country entrepreneurs, with the diaspora seen as a role model (Mayer et al., 2015). Networks offer diaspora communities invaluable and unique competitive advantages, making them fundamental to the growth and success of their own businesses, and a potential resource for harnessing entrepreneurship in their country of origin. Migrants who operate abroad often gain knowledge and skills that are lacking in the country of origin (Nielsen and Riddle, 2010). When they return to invest or start a new business, they remit this acquired human capital back to the origin country, thereby turning 'brain drain' into 'brain gain' (Saxenian, 1999; Stark, 2004).

2.3.4. Emotional Attachment as a Driver of Returnee Entrepreneurship

Emotions, both trait and state emotions, shape the evaluations of entrepreneurs as they influence how individuals process information and how they act (Foo, 2011; Welpe et al., 2012). Trait emotions are individual tendencies to feel particular emotions, while state emotions result from events eliciting particular emotions. The impact of emotion may be especially significant in circumstances characterised by high uncertainty and high engagement, as individuals may use feelings as cues for preferred courses of actions (Baron, 2008). The environment in which entrepreneurs operate is frequently unpredictable with rapid changes, and in such environments emotions can tip the balance towards activity (Foo, 2011). Although there is no interdisciplinary accepted definition of emotion (Welpe et al., 2012), we follow Cardon et al. (2012) to denote the general phenomenon of subjective feelings; with specific emotions being intense, short-lived affective reactions to specific stimuli, while moods or emotional states are low intensity, diffuse, and relatively enduring affective reactions to general stimuli. Therefore, in this chapter we use *emotion* to encompass these different types of subjective feelings, yet also go beyond this by showing how emotions lead to ties between host and home countries, with entrepreneurs gaining an impetus to act in their homeland due to this tie. As Doern and Goss (2013) state, studies on entrepreneurial emotions tend to examine how emotions shape individual preferences or behaviours, rather than examining how they are *influenced by* or *impact on* their actions. The emotional ties of returnee entrepreneurs are influenced by the context in which their activity takes place, their perceptions of the effectiveness of the institutional environment, and how this influences their investment activity. Much of the research on emotions examines negative reactions, for example associated with business failure (Shepherd, 2004; Byrne and Shepherd, 2015), with much less known about positive emotions which act as a spur to action (Welpe et al., 2012). We show that the positive emotion born out of connection to the homeland is tempered by negative emotions associated with operating in a risky and fragile institutional environment. It is the interplay of these positive and negative emotions which will determine if investments are made.

Van de Laar and de Neubourg (2006, p. 207) state that 'emotions are largely absent in economic models [of investment]' and for this reason 'many theories fail to explain the actual decisions'. However, studies of diaspora communities show that emotional ties and feelings of altruism may play a key role in deciding to conduct entrepreneurial activity in their homeland (Nkongolo-Bakenda and Chrysostome, 2013; Martinez et al., 2015). Nielsen and Riddle (2010) suggest that individual diaspora members may be motivated by the expectation of feeling significant emotional satisfaction when contemplating investment. Altruistic behaviour can be undertaken with the intention to benefit other people, but is also driven by personal desire (Snyder and Lopez, 2007; Elo, 2016). As such, diaspora entrepreneurs can be motivated to invest by the expectation of an emotional return, which can be either a 'warm glow' (Arrow, 1972) or a 'psychic income' (Michelson et al., 2004). This can lead to investments being made in socially productive activities, where resources are not allocated solely to maximise profits (Zivin and Small, 2005).

Emotional ties may be particularly strong in post-conflict economies, where an altruistic desire to improve the home country is borne out of the problems of the past. Because of their emotional ties, diaspora entrepreneurs can be motivated to invest in unstable environments that other investors consider to be too risky (Nkongolo-Bakenda and Chrysostome, 2013). In such economies, diaspora entrepreneurs can perceive their investment as a contribution to future stability and development, and as a way of helping those living in the home country (Nielsen and Riddle, 2010). Emotional ties are evident in the provision of remittances from diaspora communities to their homeland (Martinez et al., 2015). A desire to help friends and family at home leads to a regular flow of remittances, which can also assist in improving economic stability, reducing poverty rates by enabling their family members to meet consumption needs, and can facilitate human capital formation by enabling higher expenditure on education and health, as well as supporting entrepreneurial activity (Gillespie et al., 1999; Vaaler, 2013). However, despite the often large volumes of remittances, their benefit for economic growth has been called into question, with Brinkerhoff (2016) stating that they are primarily household transfers, providing income that is often essential to sustenance but could be applied for a variety of purposes, including conspicuous consumption. As such, while policy has often focused on the economic potential of remittances as part of the emotional investment of diaspora entrepreneurs, increasingly they are being seen as insufficient, and there is a need to increase the level of entrepreneurial activity if economic development is to be improved through diaspora communities. In order to do this, it is important not just to examine the economic flows into the homeland, but also the motivations behind this activity and investment, including emotional ties.

2.4. Conclusion

This chapter has shown how the role of the entrepreneur has been resurgent in theories of economic growth, although the notion of the entrepreneur, as well as the contribution of entrepreneurship to economic growth, has been widely interpreted. The theoretical approaches taken to understanding entrepreneurship highlight the importance of the dynamic and competitive markets that allow entrepreneurship to emerge. In competitive markets, entrepreneurs will be alert to opportunities which lead to the establishment of new, potentially innovative businesses. While much of the literature points to a dualism between opportunity and necessity, as well as profit versus social entrepreneurship, the chapter shows that motivations are more complex, and are largely dependent on the place in which activity is taking place. The embeddedness of entrepreneurs will determine the type of entrepreneurship that takes place as well as its potential impact. As geographical location is important for the transmission of tacit knowledge and innovation, so the role of space is important in determining entrepreneurial activity and alertness. Entrepreneurship has a pronounced geographical dimension, with differences in national start-up rates, the success of start-ups, and entrepreneurial attitudes all indicating the role of space and place in fostering entrepreneurship.

Such insights are important in examining not only entrepreneurship within borders, but also entrepreneurship that takes place across borders. Returnee entrepreneurs are subject to similar complex motivational pushes and pulls as indigenous entrepreneurs. Diaspora communities spread around the world can return to their homeland and fill valuable entrepreneurial gaps. While in many cases such return activity can be positive and is being supported by policy efforts to harness its impact, the role and potential for such returnee entrepreneurship is not clear cut. Many of these returnees can be attracted home due to an emotional attachment, rather than the quality of investment opportunities which exist at home. Examining such complexities therefore furthers understanding of returnee entrepreneurship. In the next chapter, the importance of context is explored. The chapter illustrates the importance of the institutional environment in determining entrepreneurial activity and the impact that this has on returnee entrepreneurs.

3

Returnee Entrepreneurship and Institutions

3.1. Introduction

The previous chapter set out the role of entrepreneurship in economic development. It demonstrated how entrepreneurship is widely regarded as an engine of economic growth and examined the potential for returnee entrepreneurship to contribute to homeland development. Such entrepreneurship does not occur in a vacuum, as it occurs within the institutional context. This not only impacts entrepreneurial activity within national borders, but also influences the willingness of entrepreneurs outside of a country to invest (Riddle et al., 2010). If the institutional framework is seen as problematic, investment will be discouraged. On the other hand, where institutions are stable and supportive, investment will be encouraged.

The changing and dynamic institutional environments associated with post-conflict economies (Williams and Vorley, 2017) may prove daunting and intimidating for even the most experienced entrepreneurs. This will hold back investment from the diaspora, who may view the weak institutional environment as a significant barrier. Furthermore, the diaspora can compare problematic institutions at home with the more stable and supportive environments they have experienced in their host country, analysing and making decisions based on these differences.

In order to understand the role that institutions play in harnessing or hindering return entrepreneurship, this chapter first defines institutions and discusses their evolution over time. It then sets out the particular challenges associated with institutional development in post-conflict economies, including how this will impact the intentions of returnee entrepreneurs. The chapter then provides an analysis of the institutional contexts of B&H, Kosovo, and Montenegro, drawing out implications for other challenging institutional environments.

The Diaspora and Returnee Entrepreneurship. Nick Williams, Oxford University Press (2021). © Oxford University Press.
DOI: 10.1093/oso/9780190911874.003.0003

3.2. The Importance of Institutions

While exact definitions of what constitutes institutions differ, there is a broad consensus that they include both frameworks of specific rules that regulate behaviour (e.g. laws which govern economic activity), referred to as formal institutions, and common and shared understandings (e.g. cultures, norms, and values), referred to as informal institutions. The nature of institutions and institutional arrangements serve to define the institutional context and shape economic and social outcomes. In this way, institutions provide both meaning and context to actions and activities. The entrepreneurial capacity of a nation is often defined in terms of formal institutions within a country (North, 1990); however, informal institutions are just as important (Williams and Vorley, 2015). Also, while formal and informal institutions are often examined separately, it is the interaction between the two which is crucial for economic development. Indeed, the interplay between formal and informal institutions is of critical importance in enabling and constraining entrepreneurial activity, as well as determining the nature of entrepreneurial productivity.

Institutions evolve over time as rules and perceptions change. In this sense, they are not linear. As Brinkerhoff (2016) states, much of the literature on institutional reform presumes a controlled, linear process. Yet institutional frameworks are complex and change over time, sometimes rapidly (Williams and Vorley, 2015). Indeed, this chapter will demonstrate that in post-conflict environments, large shifts have occurred in the prevailing institutions. These newborn economies have experienced 'path break' and subsequently 'path creation' as they have tried to create new institutional environments, unconnected to the institutional arrangements of the past. This has implications for economic and social development, as well as for indigenous and returnee entrepreneurship.

3.2.1. Formal Institutions

Formal institutions are the rules and regulations which are written down or formally accepted, and give guidance to the economic and legal framework of a country (Krasniqi and Desai, 2016). Where formal institutions are strong and well-enforced, over time entrepreneurial activity can be fostered and in turn contribute to economic growth (Acs et al., 2008). However, where formal institutions are weak, they can impose costly bureaucratic burdens on entrepreneurs, and this increases uncertainty as well as the operational and transaction costs of firms (Puffer et al., 2010).

Developed economies are often characterised as having stable institutional environments, which supports business start-up and growth. The United States is often cited as the exemplar of a low-regulation economy, with formal institutions enabling entrepreneurial activity. Celebratory odes to the entrepreneurial titans of Silicon Valley loom large in the public understanding of entrepreneurship. This has influenced policy elsewhere, for example in the European Union, where the Lisbon Strategy attempted to create a 'friendly environment' for starting and developing a business, and which had the implicit desire to shift the European economy to be more like that of the United States (Atherton, 2006). Yet despite this exemplar status, the latest data from the World Bank's 'Doing Business Survey', which measures various aspects of formal institutions, including the ease of starting a business, access to credit, property rights, and payment of taxes, finds that New Zealand has the most efficient formal institutional environment. The United States is ranked sixth, ahead of the United Kingdom in eighth place (World Bank, 2019).

The ease of starting a business is a simple method for measuring formal institutions, although it obviously does not capture the complexity of the formal institutional environment. Nevertheless, a positive link has been identified between economic growth and entrepreneurship in developed economies where it is easy to start a business, while the same relationship has not been established for developing economies (Sautet, 2013). A key reason for this is explained by the lack of effective formal institutions in developing economies (Williams and Vorley, 2015). Entrepreneurs in weak formal institutional environments, for example in transition economies which have moved from centralised planning to more open market conditions, can often be faced with incoherent and/or constantly changing regulations (Manolova and Yan, 2002; Aidis et al., 2008), meaning that they are not able to plan effectively (Tonoyan et al., 2010). While a stable legal framework with well-protected property rights can promote planning and coordination, as well as prevent the ad hoc expropriation of the fruits of entrepreneurship (Henrekson, 2007), the experience in many developing economies has been that the legal system has been incapable of adequately enforcing laws and of resolving business disputes (Manolova and Yan, 2002). This is despite many former centrally planned economies having adopted legal frameworks similar to those of more developed economies, including laws relating to property, bankruptcy, contracts, and taxes; however, they have been inefficient in implementing them (Smallbone and Welter, 2001; Aidis et al., 2008). Due to these inefficiencies, going to court to settle a business dispute can be both time-consuming and costly. In addition, perceptions that the institutions are often corrupt means that many entrepreneurs will avoid turning to the courts to settle disputes

(Tonoyan et al., 2010). In such environments, entrepreneurs will often instead use informal networks to compensate for the weakness (or failures) of formal institutions, for example by using connections to bend the rules or paying bribes that break them (Aidis and Adachi, 2007). Another challenge is gaining credit in such economies, as banks favour larger businesses and lack the willingness to finance small enterprises (Smallbone and Welter, 2001). Accessing credit is a major constraining factor for entrepreneurial activity in transition countries, and as a resort small firms often either have to turn to the informal credit network, for example borrowing money from family and friends, or bribing bureaucrats to secure access to capital (Guseva, 2007).

3.2.2. Informal Institutions

While business start-ups are often used as a proxy for entrepreneurship, they only represent one of the many outcomes of entrepreneurial activity (Huggins and Williams, 2009). The phenomenon of entrepreneurship is largely a phenomenon of the mind, concerning alertness to opportunity, perception, and imagination (Kirzner, 1973), and is a behavioural characteristic of individuals expressed through innovative attributes, flexibility, and adaptability to change (Swedberg, 2000). As Sautet and Kirzner (2006, p. 17) suggest, culture shapes 'what an individual perceives as opportunities and thus what he overlooks, as entrepreneurship is always embedded in a cultural context'. As a result, culture plays a key role in fostering entrepreneurship (Huggins and Williams, 2009). Yet despite its importance to economic development, what constitutes culture is often vague (Olson, 2007). However, through examination of informal institutions it is possible to understand the prevalent norms and values which enable and constrain entrepreneurial cultures.

Informal institutions can be defined as traditions, customs, societal norms, culture, and unwritten codes of conduct (Baumol, 1990; North, 1990; Smallbone et al., 2010). The presence of these within a society define and determine models of individual behaviour based on subjectivity and meanings that affect beliefs and actions (Bruton et al., 2010). Such norms and values are the often taken-for-granted culturally specific behaviours that are learned living or growing up in a given community or society, and they engender a predictability of behaviour in social interactions. Over time, these norms and values are reinforced by a system of rewards and sanctions to ensure compliance and themselves become an informal institutions (DiMaggio and Powell, 1983).

Understanding informal institutions is important to entrepreneurship in terms of how societies accept entrepreneurs, inculcate values, and create a cultural milieu whereby entrepreneurship is accepted and encouraged (Bruton et al., 2010). Indeed informal institutions are widely acknowledged as critical to explaining different levels of entrepreneurial activity across countries (Frederking, 2004; Puffer et al., 2010). Understanding informal institutions represents a substantive challenge for academics and policy makers alike, as affecting cultural change demands a clear understanding as to the intended objectives of such interventions and the mechanisms by which they are achieved. Where informal institutions within a society are not well understood or adequately considered by policy makers, then institutional reforms will have a limited overall impact on fostering entrepreneurship.

More developed open economies are often considered to have informal institutions that are supportive of entrepreneurship, with norms and values that are supportive of pursuing entrepreneurial opportunities and that view entrepreneurial activity positively. Common examples such as Silicon Valley and Route 128 in Boston demonstrate how, through shared norms and values, an entrepreneurial culture can be both fostered and sustained (Saxenian, 1996). By contrast, developing economies often lack the norms and values which are considered to create positive entrepreneurial cultures in more developed economies. The demise of socialist systems in Eastern Europe and the former Soviet Union have seen dramatic changes in political, economic, and juridical institutions. However, the many norms and values in these transitional economies learned and adopted during the socialist years remained engrained and largely unchanged (Vorley and Williams, 2016a). Indeed, Winiecki (2001) states that modern history offers no better field to test the interaction of changing formal rules and prevailing informal rules than Eastern European and the former Soviet Union. These countries are characterised by informal institutions which have substituted for, rather than complementing, changes in the formal institutional environment (Guseva, 2007; Estrin and Prevezer, 2011). Moreover, in environments with un(der)reformed and weak formal institutions, such as transition economies, entrepreneurial activity is typically guided and governed by informal codes of conduct (Ahlstrom and Bruton, 2010). As a result, existing research has shown that entrepreneurial behaviours in many transition economies are often shaped by the informal institutions inherited from socialist regimes, with unwritten codes, norms, and social conventions dominating everyday practice (Ledeneva, 1998).

Reforms in developing economies often focus on formal institutions (Manolova and Yan, 2002). In transition economies, liberalisation was expected to create new and numerous opportunities for entrepreneurship (Saar and Unt, 2008). Yet often there has not been a corresponding shift in informal institutions, which has stymied entrepreneurship (Williams and Vorley,

2015). In many ways, reforms to the formal environment are undertaken with little or no consideration as to the depth and importance of informal institutions. While reforming informal institutions is possible, it is often a slow process, since the norms and values passed from one generation to the next can be resistant to change (Winiecki, 2001). As Estrin and Mickiewicz (2011) state, changes in informal institutions can take a full generation to occur. It is important to note, however, that there are some examples of successful changes to informal institutions. For example, Georgia's institutions have changed, leading to improvements in their World Bank 'Doing Business' rankings (World Bank, 2016), while at the same time perceptions of opportunity have improved, with social values towards entrepreneurship higher than in many EU and non-EU countries (Global Entrepreneurship Monitor, 2015). Similarly, post-conflict economies have seen shifts in their informal institutions, with societal perceptions of entrepreneurship becoming more positive (Williams and Vorley, 2017).

As entrepreneurship becomes more visible and valued in society, it gains legitimation, and the growth of entrepreneurial attitudes, ambition, and perspectives in turn serves to reinforce the emergence of a positive entrepreneurial culture (Minniti, 2005). In this sense, although government is clearly important in shaping the institutional environment and influencing entrepreneurial activity (Smallbone and Welter, 2001; Acs et al., 2008), the remit for institutional change is beyond the purview of policy makers alone, although they too can help foster a more entrepreneurial culture (Williams and Vorley, 2015). Entrepreneurs themselves can also act as change agents and influence the institutional landscape (McMullen, 2011). Culturally, entrepreneurship is reinforced by informal institutions as individuals follow social norms and are influenced by what others have chosen to do. Therefore in order to reform informal institutions and promote a more entrepreneurial culture, Verheul et al. (2001) refer to the importance of a positive feedback cycle whereby people see others succeeding as entrepreneurial activity and are motivated to be more entrepreneurial. In consequence, over time, informal institutions can be influenced and improved, and entrepreneurs' actions can contribute to wider societal change and economic development (Welter and Smallbone, 2011).

3.2.3. The Importance of Institutional Alignment

Ensuring the complementarity, or alignment, of formal and informal institutions is important in promoting entrepreneurship (Williams and Vorley, 2017). As institutions evolve, the interplay and relationship between the formal and informal are critical if entrepreneurship is to be supported. Where the formal and informal complement each other, entrepreneurial activity will be fostered; conversely, where there is asymmetry, entrepreneurial activity will be stymied (Williams and Vorley, 2015). The extant literature on institutions argues that formal and informal institutions interact in two key ways, with formal institutions either supporting (i.e. complementing) or undermining (i.e. substituting) informal institutions (North, 1990; Tonoyan et al., 2010; Estrin and Prevezer, 2011). Informal institutions are complementary if they create and strengthen incentives to comply with the formal institutions, and thereby plug gaps in problems of social interaction, thus enhancing the efficiency of formal institutions (Baumol, 1990; North, 1990). Where informal institutions substitute for formal institutions, individual incentives are structured in such a way that they are incompatible with formal institutions, and this often exists in environments where the formal institutions are weak or not enforced (Estrin and Prevezer, 2011). The interactions between formal and informal institutions present a key challenge for policy makers who seek to foster entrepreneurship by changing the 'rules of the game' and the prevalent culture.

Economic growth will be held back when formal and informal institutions are not aligned. This occurs when the formal rules do not reflect the informal norms of conduct and vice versa. In such cases, formal institutions cannot be enforced properly, and the informal norms take priority, thus making enforcement of rules difficult and costly. Formal institutions only affect people if they are enforced; otherwise the asymmetry can result in rules and regulations being circumvented by informal institutions (Williams and Vorley, 2015). Figure 3.1 depicts how formal institutions are costly to enforce, while informal institutions are self-enforced. Where there is overlap between the two, formal rules and informal norms complement each other, and are thus easy to enforce.

Williamson (2009) demonstrates how institutions operate at different levels and influence each other, with informal institutions often emerging spontaneously yet influenced by the calculative construction of formal rules. Formal rules are mediated by interaction with informal norms, and the economic outcomes of these interactions change over time (Winiecki, 2001), with norms affecting how rules are designed and implemented and whether they are followed. Institutional asymmetry can be caused by a misalignment between formal and informal institutions (Williams et al., 2017a). The asymmetry can develop over time as formal institutions are reformed to support entrepreneurship while informal institutions remain unsupportive; or changes in informal institutions remain incompatible with formal institutions.

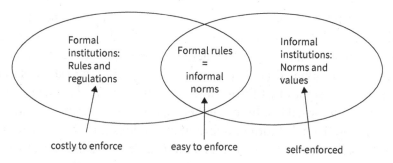

Figure 3.1 Overlap between formal and informal institutions.
Source: Williams et al. (2017a).

Alternatively, asymmetry can reduce over time if the incongruence improves. We posit that ensuring the complementarity, or alignment, of formal and informal institutions has been identified in the literature as important in promoting entrepreneurship. The asymmetry or alignment between formal and informal institutions takes different forms and has differential impacts depending on the level of economic development in a country, as well as the policy priorities followed.

3.2.4. Productive, Unproductive, and Destructive Entrepreneurship

Chapter 2 introduced Baumol's (1990) theory of the distribution between productive, unproductive, and destructive entrepreneurial activities. This theory is important for understanding the differences between entrepreneurship in stable economies compared to those that are more turbulent. Productive entrepreneurship can be understood as activities that benefit the entrepreneur and society at large; it is important to an economy because it is the fundamental source of economic growth and wealth creation (Sobel, 2008). Unproductive entrepreneurship consists of activities which benefit the entrepreneur but harm society at large, while destructive activities destroy economic capacity, such as land, labour, or capital (Baumol, 1990). The distribution between productive, unproductive, and destructive entrepreneurship is affected by institutional arrangements and the social payoff structure, with the 'rules of the game' developing over time (North, 1990). This stresses the importance of understanding economic development in its historical context, as the institutions which develop will play a key role in determining whether entrepreneurship is productive, unproductive, or destructive.

Baumol (1990) exemplifies this through analyses of ancient Rome, medieval China, and England in the Middle Ages. He finds that the institutional structure in ancient Rome was weighted towards a culture pursuing wealth through landholding, usury, and political moneymaking, rather than involvement in industry or commerce; that although China was technologically advanced, the economy remained stagnant due to the continuous curtailment of economic activity by government; and that in England, a period of sustainable economic growth lasting centuries was seen as resulting in the incentives being weighted towards productive entrepreneurship (Baumol, 1990). These insights allow the analysis of institutional frameworks to aid understanding of how they influence entrepreneurial activity.

Baumol's theory has implications for government intervention to promote entrepreneurship, as he argues that unproductive activities can be incentivised by 'rent seeking' for government support and funds (Baumol, 1990). As an example, he highlights Japan, where compared to the United States the rules of the game have discouraged the allocation of entrepreneurial talent into rent-seeking litigation (Baumol, 1990). This insight has relevance for contemporary entrepreneurship policy, as the presence of support and funding for entrepreneurs creates a rent for entrepreneurs to seek, and successful enterprises may seek to protect themselves from competition by gaining government favours and protection (Sobel et al., 2007). This will cause some entrepreneurs to move away from previously productive activities (which satisfied consumer desires and led to economic growth) to engage in unproductive activities.

Instead of direct support, Baumol's theory suggests that by facilitating and stimulating business start-up, especially through reducing barriers to entry, policy makers can promote competition and guard against monopoly formation (Baumol, 1990). As Sobel (2008 653) affirms, rather than intervention, 'the better path is through institutional reform that constrains or minimises government's role, lowering the return to unproductive entrepreneurship [as] government programmes too often encourage entrepreneurial individuals to devote effort toward figuring out how to obtain the transfers, rather than devoting those efforts toward satisfying consumers and creating wealth'. Such insights allow institutions to be 'observed, described, and, with luck, modified and improved' (Baumol, 1990, p. 894).

3.3. Institutions in Post-Conflict Economies

Transition economies have generally experienced path extension with respect to their institutions (Hashi and Krasniqi, 2011). This has seen previous institutional arrangements adapted with varying degrees of success, while informal institutions have been slow to change (Manolova and Yan, 2002; Tonoyan et al., 2010; Estrin and Mickiewicz, 2011). However, other countries which have seen political change happen quickly, such as newborn, post-conflict economies, can be understood as having experienced 'path break' and subsequently new 'path creation'.

Creating institutions which can foster entrepreneurship, and with it deliver socio-economic development and transformation in post-conflict environments, represents a particular challenge. There are immediate issues associated with embedding and enforcing newly established formal institutions, while in path dependence terms the extension of prevailing informal institutions simultaneously serves to undermine these reforms due to the substitutive effect. For entrepreneurs in post-conflict environments, navigating new formal institutional frameworks can be challenging, and this can be exacerbated where there is a resistance to entrepreneurial activity which is viewed as individualistic and contrary to socialist norms. Efendic et al. (2015) also note that where the social fabric has been damaged, the level of trust is low and people are unwilling to share knowledge. This can further stymie entrepreneurial endeavours. Moreover, internal conflicts can undermine the rule of law, which is a critical element of institutions as weak rules increase the risk of expropriation of entrepreneurial returns (Estrin et al., 2016), with it being replaced by local informal structures of power such as criminal groups (Armakolas, 2011), which are likely to leave a legacy of institutional asymmetries after the conflict has ceased (Efendic et al., 2015). In transition economies, such as the independent states created following the break-up of the Soviet Union, many of the informal institutions continued to persist in keeping with socialist ideologies and to exert influence in the newly liberalised transition economies (Williams and Vorley, 2015). Consequently, any effort to develop formal institutions were undermined by the persistence of informal institutions (i.e. the substitutionary effect). Again, this emphasises the need to examine not only formal and informal institutions, but also their interaction, if the implications for entrepreneurship are to be understood.

Post-conflict newborn states face different institutional challenges to other post-socialist transition economies. The creation of a new state arising from conflict has provided the foundations to create new formal institutions, but has also been a catalyst to an ideological shift in informal institutions away from those norms and values of the former Serbian regime and towards those associated with Western democracies (notably the United States). This break and reorientation of informal institutions is born out of efforts to rebuild fragile economies, and positive institutional reforms can provide a significant opportunity for growth (Efendic et al., 2015).

As has been illustrated, perceptions of institutions are important, as expectations are self-fulfilling. Where expectations are of a stable environment, institutions will gain legitimacy and enhance compliance (Crawford and Ostrom, 1995). On the other hand, where expectations are of a changing environment which lacks stability, individuals can seek to circumvent rules or not risk undertaking entrepreneurial activity (Williams and Vorley, 2015). In economies with weak or negative perceptions and expectations, informal institutions will take time to change (Winiecki, 2001; Estrin and Mickiewicz, 2011) but can be targeted through media campaigns, education, and utilisation of role models (Hindle and Klyver, 2007; Williams and Vorley, 2015). Analogous to this, there is a need to develop the ambition and capabilities of entrepreneurs in order to foster more productive and systemic entrepreneurship, which will in turn increase the complementarity of formal and informal institutions. This focus on developing and embedding institutions is particularly critical given the geopolitical challenges facing post-conflict economies, as further political marginalisation will undoubtedly constrain opportunities for entrepreneurship.

As Bruck et al. (2013) state, understanding how institutions can shape the incentives of individuals to engage in entrepreneurial activities is of critical importance in conflict and post-conflict economies. This matters for indigenous entrepreneurs who have stayed within their home country despite conflict (see, for example, Collier and Duponchel, 2013; Sanders and Weitzel, 2013) as well as returnee entrepreneurs.

In order to ensure that returnee entrepreneurs are mobilised and willing to invest in their home countries, it is important that the institutional environment is supportive and stable. Institutions refer to the constraints designed by people to structure interactions (North, 1990), and these constraints can shape incentives for market actors, such as by shaping predicted rewards and risks (Krasniqi and Desai, 2016; Williams et al., 2017a). Post-conflict economies are often characterised by weak formal institutions and informal institutions which are unsupportive of entrepreneurial activity. Where formal institutions reduce risks and ensure stability, they will generate trust (Busenitz et al., 2000). Such regulations assign property rights (Spencer and Gomez, 2004) and where these are poorly defined or not enforced, the risk of expropriation of entrepreneurial returns is increased (Estrin et al., 2016). Where such expropriation exists, productive entrepreneurs can see assets liquidated, their venture terminated, and the proceeds consumed by others (Desai et al., 2013). As a result, trust in institutions will decline.

Where entrepreneurs are subject to uncertainty, in the form of changing regulations, the bureaucracy and the cost of compliance can impose increased operational and transaction costs, and increase the risks associated with entrepreneurial activity (Tonoyan et al., 2010). In environments with frequent changes in laws, rules, and regulations, uncertainty is created, meaning that entrepreneurs are less able to plan for the future, and the costs of compliance increase, thereby redirecting resources which could be invested in growth activities (Williams and Vorley, 2015). Volatility in the formal institutional environment can be hostile to firm growth and can increase the risks associated with activity as anticipations of future profits are affected (Krasniqi and Desai, 2016). This is especially salient in developing economies, where institutional change can be faster and less predictable than in mature market economies, and also in post-conflict economies where formal institutions are being established (Nielsen and Riddle, 2010). In addition, given that diaspora entrepreneurs have significant international experience, they are able to compare the relative stability of the institutional environment in their host country with the instability of their home country.

Although returnee entrepreneurs are often the first foreign investors moving into uncertain political and economic climates (Gillespie et al., 2001), such activity may be stymied where there is a lack of trust. Where the social fabric has been damaged, the level of trust is low and people may be unwilling to share knowledge, which can hold back entrepreneurial endeavours (Efendic et al., 2015). Institutional trust is a critical element in fostering productive entrepreneurial activity (Anokhin and Schulze, 2009) and entrepreneurial intentions (Lajqi and Krasniqi, 2017), and where trust is lacking, international migrants can simply chose to remain abroad. In countries undergoing significant change, such as post-conflict economies, trust in institutions is not likely to be immediate and will take time to develop (Krasniqi and Desai, 2016). Furthermore, the institutional environment may lead to more destructive entrepreneurship, as issues such as corruption shift incentives for entrepreneurs, encouraging them to seek short-term payoffs determined by shorter time horizons (Desai et al., 2013).

Overcoming a lack of trust is a key element in harnessing entrepreneurial intentions towards the homeland. Intentions are the first step in a typically long-term process of starting a new business (Krueger, 1993; Thompson, 2009). Understanding what drives entrepreneurial intentions in adverse conditions, for example post-conflict economies, can assist in the design of (more) effective institutions to support entrepreneurial endeavours (Bullough et al., 2014). To launch a venture even in a stable and supportive environment, individuals require self-efficacy, which is associated with opportunity recognition and risk-taking (Krueger et al., 2000). In post-conflict economies, self-efficacy can support entrepreneurial intentions, but if these are to be realised they must overcome the perceptions of risk. As such, institutions must lead to improved trust and perceptions of risk. Navigating institutional frameworks is always challenging, but particularly so for returnee entrepreneurs who may never have lived in the home country, have lived abroad for a number of years, or who know relatively few people in the country (Nielsen and Riddle, 2010).

3.4. Institutional Change and Returnee Entrepreneurship

Figure 3.2 demonstrates the interplay between institutional change in the home country and returnee entrepreneurial activity. In emerging and post-conflict economies, returnees can be involved in the creation of new firms

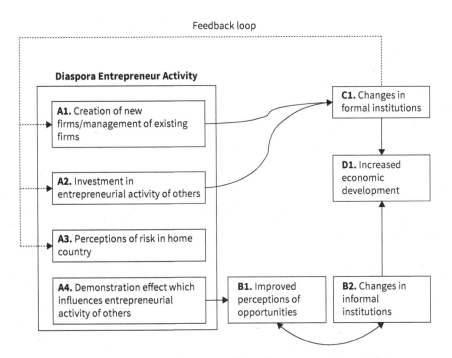

Figure 3.2 Impacts of returnee entrepreneurship on home country institutions.
Source: World Bank (2017).

and/or management of existing firms (A1), as well as investment in entrepreneurial activity of others (A2). Yet a key barrier to this activity is the perception of risk associated with an underdeveloped institutional environment (A3). Returnees will respond by minimising risks when investing, yet their engagement can also be an impetus for changes to formal institutions. As stated in Chapter 1, this is not caused by returnee entrepreneurs seeking to directly change institutions themselves, but rather by the responses of government policy makers seeking to improve institutions so that the investments of returnees can be maximised. If formal institutions are improved, more entrepreneurial activity and investment can be created, and this then provides opportunity for policy makers to make further institutional changes to harness higher levels of economic activity.

In less developed and post-conflict economies, policy makers are seeking to increasingly involve diaspora in policy making so that positive changes can be made, and to ensure that there is an effective feedback loop between the diaspora and institutional change (Riddle and Brinkerhoff, 2011; Kshetri, 2013). The changes in formal institutions create a feedback loop (C1) which fosters further entrepreneurial activity through improvements in perceptions of risk. At the same time, entrepreneurial activity by returnees influences those in their home country through a demonstration effect (A4). Returnee entrepreneurs act as role models, which encourages others into entrepreneurial action through improved perceptions of opportunity (B1). This improves the perceptions of home-based entrepreneurs of the institutional environment, thereby changing the norms and values associated with informal institutions (B2), and has a two-way effect as improvements in informal institutions lead to a positive impact on activity. Improvements in both formal and informal institutions, and the increased entrepreneurial activity that results, in turn can increase economic development (D1).

3.5. The Contexts of Bosnia and Herzegovina, Kosovo, and Montenegro

The empirical focus of this book is the newborn, post-conflict economies of B&H, Kosovo, and Montenegro. Each of these economies have experienced 'path break' and subsequently 'path creation' as they have tried to create new institutional environments, unconnected to the Yugoslav past. As previously semi-autonomous regions within Yugoslavia, they possessed varying degrees of policy making power, and all of them lacked national rules and regulations by which to govern economic activity. Each of the former Yugoslav republics is forging its own institutional paths (Xheneti and Kitching, 2011; Efendic et al., 2015), while at the same time attempting to come to terms with their recent conflict-affected past. As previously semi-autonomous regions within Yugoslavia, they possessed varying degrees of policy making power. The majority of rules were imposed centrally by Belgrade. All of the newborn countries lacked autonomy over the rules and regulations with which to govern economic activity.

The backdrop of war is important to understanding institutional development in each of these economies. War has influenced politics and wider society, and continues to have lasting effects in terms of relationships with neighbours and also within countries. The long shadow of war can be exemplified by the conviction for war crimes of Bosnian Serb leader Ratko Mladic at the International Criminal Tribunal for the former Yugoslavia (ICTY) in 2017. The charge sheet against Mladic was long, with his involvement in the Srebrenica massacre perhaps the most widely covered in the media. Mladic's conviction was greeted with relief in the Bosniak Federation and elsewhere in the former Yugoslavia, with people pleased that a dark period of the past could be at least partly consigned to history. However, in the Serb-dominated Republika Srpska, politicians as well as members of the public were quick to condemn the decision, with many celebrating Mladic as a war hero. Similarly, the naming of a student dormitory in honour of the Bosnian Serb leader Radovan Karadicz, and unveiled by Milorad Dodik, president of the Republika Srpska, prior to his sentence for 11 counts of war crimes, is symbolic of the tensions which remain between the majority Serb and majority Bosniak areas and which hamper effective bilateral policy. In Kosovo, there have been political frictions relating to the redrawing of the border with Serbia, and continued tensions in the north of the country which have occasionally spilled over into violence. In Montenegro, there has been continued controversy regarding previous ties with Serbia following the end of war, and subsequent independence, as well as continued political fallout, for example related to accusations of an alleged attempted coup fomented by Russia in 2017 as the country seeks closer ties to the European Union.

3.5.1. Coming Out of Conflict

The breakdown of the communist regime in the early 1990s was the beginning of the end of 'old Yugoslavia', despite several unsuccessful military campaigns to unite Serbia with neighbouring republics into a 'Greater Serbia' (Glenny, 1996; Judah, 2008). NATO intervention and the conclusion of the wars ultimately led to the break-up of the former Yugoslavia and the creation of a number of newly independent states.

Bosnia and Herzegovina declared independence from Yugoslavia on 1 March 1992, and a bitter ethnic war raged until 1995. Media coverage of the Srebrenica massacre and the Siege of Sarajevo, which lasted over three years, exemplified the atrocities carried out throughout the country. The legacy of conflict is one of a divided country, and B&H is now home to one of the world's most complicated systems of government, which began with the Dayton Accords that brought the war to a conclusion. At the first level, there is the predominantly Bosniak Federation and the Serb-dominated Republika Srpska, as well as the self-governing administrative unit of Brcko; at the second level, there are 10 cantons, and the third has over 100 municipalities. Dayton achieved its immediate purpose of putting an end to the bloodshed, but it froze its ethnic divisions in place. The accords bequeathed an extremely complex system of government, which has made governance extremely difficult, as ethnic tensions pose a challenge for economic and social development. On a number of measures, B&H failed to place itself on a path toward growth and development (Cowen and Coyne, 2005).

This complicated system of government presents a real challenge for developing policy aimed at fostering social cohesion and economic growth. However, different rules exist in the Federation and Republika Srpska, which means that there are different economic outcomes. Integration across political entities is not straightforward, with common agreements on regulation, taxation, and trade fraught with political challenges. Since the end of the war, political allegiances have largely been based on ethnic identities which remain entrenched.

The war in B&H led to the displacement of people outside of the country and also within (Eastmond, 2006). As Halilovich (2012) states, this displacement revived traditional local and ethnic identities within the country, as well as producing new categories of individuals, including 'stayers' and 'leavers', 'newcomers' and 'old settlers', 'defenders' and 'deserters', internally displaced persons (IDPs) and refugees. B&H changed from a country of ethnic diversity to ethnic homogeneity in some areas (Efendic et al., 2011) and where the three main ethnic groups (Bosniaks, Serbs, and Croats) have substantial autonomy and control over their own ethno-territorial units (Bieber, 2010).

Kosovo was previously part of Yugoslavia and then Serbia, and the war of 1998–1999 served to further damage its already fragile economy. Following the continuation of political and ethnic tensions after the end of the war, Kosovo unilaterally declared its independence as a new state in 2008, albeit with continued tensions in parts of the country (Ivlevs and King, 2012a;

Williams and Vorley, 2017). The country is characterised by high levels of insecurity (Hoxha, 2009) and, in common with Collier's (2007) identification of a development trap being 'landlocked with bad neighbours', it suffers from political marginalisation given that it is not recognised by some other countries, including neighbouring Serbia.

As a result of the Kosovo war, some 800,000 people out of a population of 1.8 million were forced to flee the country; another 400,000 were forced to flee their homes and hide within Kosovo; 10,000 people were killed, and 3,000 were abducted (Kellezi et al., 2009). Following NATO intervention and the conclusion of the wars, the former Yugoslavia was split into different nations, including Serbia, which contained the formerly autonomous province of Kosovo. However, following the continuation of political and ethnic tensions, Kosovo unilaterally declared its independence in 2008 (Yannis, 2009; Ivlevs and King, 2012b).

Between the end of the conflict in 1999 and independence, the challenge of institutional development was the objective of the transitional UN Interim Administration Mission in Kosovo (UNMIK) under UN Resolution 1244, which stated that Kosovo would have autonomy within the Federal Republic of Yugoslavia, and aimed to develop governance arrangements for the self-administration of the country. Indeed, UNMIK was a 'state-building' operation, aiming to develop levers of power so that the country could sustain itself (Knudsen, 2010). Post-independence, Kosovo has received assistance from international agencies, including KFOR, the peacekeeping force; the European Rule of Law Mission in Kosovo (EULEX), the EU Rule of Law Mission; as well as the International Monetary Fund (IMF), United Nations and World Bank, to support institutional development. Despite some institutional progress, Kosovo remains one of the poorest states in Europe (Ivlevs and King, 2012a), and has been plagued by high unemployment, low levels of growth, high levels of poverty, and poor infrastructure (Krasniqi, 2007; Hoxha, 2009). The extent of the challenges facing Kosovo are also reflected in economic growth and income per capita figures, which are among the lowest in the Balkans (IMF, 2012).

Montenegro was part of various Yugoslav and Balkan unions for 88 years, and during the early 1990s supported the Serbian government's war aims in Croatia and B&H. As such, Montenegro was something of an accomplice to the crimes committed in its Western neighbours, yet at the same there existed a strong anti-war movement opposed to Serb nationalism (Bieber, 2003). Despite this, Montenegro maintained political ties with Serbia following the collapse of Yugoslavia. After the collapse of Yugoslavia, only two of the six constitutive republics remained together: Montenegro and Serbia. However, growing differences led to a referendum vote for independence in 2006 (Drakic et al., 2007). As such, while Montenegro felt the effects of the Yugoslav wars, these were not as pronounced as in B&H and Kosovo. In part, this has been due better inter-ethnic relations within Montenegro, which has prevented an escalation of majority-minority relations (Sistek and Dimitrovova, 2003).

Although the impact of conflict has been much less in Montenegro compared to B&H and Kosovo, it has still been required to develop new institutional arrangements as a result of its newborn status. In part due to the challenges of doing this, and developing a competitive market economy in a country with a population of around 700,000 people, it has still seen significant emigration in recent years (Federal Ministry for Economic Cooperation and Development, 2012), and economic growth has been slow.

Corruption is prevalent in each of the three countries (Belloni and Strazzari, 2014; Williams et al., 2017b). Political connections are important and can facilitate access to extensive business opportunities. Without such connections, opportunities can be cut off. The existence of corruption in B&H, Kosovo, and Montenegro has two key explanations: first, weak internal institutions which have failed to properly tackle corrupt activity; and second, the imposition of external norms from international actors which were not appropriate to local context and have created space for corruption. With regards to the first explanation, stories of corruption among key political actors and criminal organisations are well established. The rules established in the three countries have so far failed to effectively sanction the perpetrators of large-scale criminal activity, thereby allowing it to continue. This is similar to other countries, particularly the transition economies, which have failed to create institutions which can stifle corruption (Vorley and Williams, 2016a). Yet at the same time, the second explanation is an important dimension in these post-conflict economies. Following war, the international community has been greatly involved in setting economic and political agendas in the Balkans to greater or lesser degrees. This involvement has not always been successful. Economically liberal policies have been encouraged to create more open market economies, yet this has led to the privatisation of state assets in highly corrupt and secretive ways (Knudsen, 2010; Koman et al., 2015). Such approaches have meant that corruption has been legitimised by international actors who have pressured local policy makers to accept the formal architecture of good governance, which did not tackle the real contextual, on-the-ground issues (Belloni and Strazzari, 2014).

Issues such as corruption have meant that the institutional frameworks for B&H, Kosovo, and Montenegro remain highly challenging. Table 3.1 sets out the key measures of the quality of institutions in the three countries, and

Table 3.1 Measures of the Quality of the Institutional Environment in Balkan Economies

	Overall DB Rank 2017[a]	Overall DB Rank 2016[a]	Starting a Business[a]			Dealing with Construction Permits[a]			Enforcing Contracts[a]			Perception of Corruption[b] 2018 Rank
			Procedures	Days	Costs of Income per Capita	Procedures	Days	Costs of Warehouse Value	QJP	Days	Costs of Claim	
Albania	58	90	5	5	10.1%	16	220	3.3%	6	525	34.9%	99
B&H	174	175	12	65	13.5%	15	179	18.5%	11	595	36.0%	89
Croatia	43	39	8	7	7.3%	19	127	8.3%	15	572	16.7%	60
Kosovo	60	64	3	6	1.1%	15	152	6.1%	9.5	330	33.4%	93=
Macedonia	10	16	2	2	0.1%	9	89	5.1%	14	634	28.8%	93=
Montenegro	51	53	6	10	1.5%	8	152	11.3%	11.5	545	11.5%	67
Serbia	47	54	5	7	6.5%	12	156	3.2%	13	635	40.8%	87
Slovenia	49	45	4	7	0.0%	12	224.5	2.7%	10.5	1,160	12.7%	36

Sources: [a] World Bank Doing Business Report 2017 (www.doingbusiness.org, accessed: 03/05/2017); [b] Transparency International 2019 www.transparency.org, accessed: 29/01/2019.

Key: QJP: quality of judicial procedures; DB: World Bank Doing Business ranking.

compares these with other Balkan economies. The table shows that B&H has the weakest environment for doing business, and compares unfavourably to the G8 in terms of days (65) and procedures (12) to start a business. However, Kosovo and Montenegro compare much more favourably, with 6 days and 3 procedures required to start a business in Kosovo, and 10 days and 6 procedures in Montenegro. Yet in all three economies there are significant issues in terms of dealing with permits and contracts, and perceptions of corruption are generally negative. There is also significant avoidance of taxation, as well as 'off-the-books' business activities to avoid taxation or regulations. A measure of perceptions of corruption demonstrates these issues, with Kosovo performing the worst of the three countries (93rd out of 180 countries), with B&H ranked 89th and Montenegro fairing better at 67 (Transparency International, 2019).

3.5.2. The Diaspora Communities of B&H, Kosovo, and Montenegro

B&H, Kosovo, and Montenegro have all experienced high levels of unemployment and poverty, and low levels of growth, all of which have contributed to further migration (Krasniqi, 2007; Hoxha, 2009; MHRR, 2016). B&H's diaspora is estimated at approximately 2 million, equivalent to 53% of the population (MHRR, 2016); Kosovo's diaspora is estimated at approximately 700,000 people, equivalent to 40% of the resident population (United Nations Development Programme, 2014); and Montenegro's is estimated at 200,000, equivalent to 32% of the population (Government of Montenegro, 2014). During the conflict, remittances to Kosovo from emigrants accounted for 45% of annual domestic revenues (Demmers, 2007), and were in part used to support the war effort, with the Kosovo Liberation Army establishing an international 'Homeland Calling' fund (Adamson, 2006). In addition, a '3% fund' was used so that migrants contributed not only to the war, but also to support government spending on schools and hospitals (Hockenos, 2003). In the aftermath of the wars, remittances from these diaspora communities became increasingly important to the three economies, but especially in Kosovo (Loxha, 2012; Peci et al., 2012). Around a quarter of Kosovo Albanian households receive remittances from the diaspora (Kosovo Agency for Statistics, 2013; Vorley and Williams, 2016b), totalling approximately 17% of GDP, making Kosovo one of the top 15 recipients of remittances worldwide, relative to the size of the domestic economy (United Nations Development Programme, 2012). Substantial amounts of money are also poured into the economy each year through diaspora tourism, estimated at €270 million in 2012 (Kosovo Agency for Statistics, 2013). In B&H, remittances are estimated at 14% of the country's GDP, while figures for Montenegro are not currently available (Federal Ministry for Economic Cooperation and Development, 2012).

Table 3.2 shows the inflow of remittances for B&H, Kosovo, and Montenegro compared to other Balkan economies. It demonstrates that remittance flows to Montenegro are the lowest, representing the size of the diaspora as well as the size of the economy, although the amount has grown year on year from 2010 to 2017. B&H and Kosovo have seen fluctuations in the level of remittances in the same time period, although the figures for 2017 are higher than those in 2010. Serbia has the highest level of remittances in the Balkans, again representing the size of the economy and size of population.

The diaspora of B&H, Kosovo, and Montenegro all hold strong ties to their homeland, and are in a position to contribute to long-term economic and social development by investing its accumulated financial capital, transferring skills and facilitating links between their home country and larger foreign markets. However, the mobilisation of the diaspora to contribute to economic development is currently not reaching its potential, in part because of a lack of effective policy implementation and coordination. This leads to negative perceptions among the diaspora communities who view the financial risk to investments, lack of support, political fragmentation, and weak institutional framework as barriers to investment (Agunias and Newland, 2012).

While the three countries all have large diasporas which are spread around the world, particularly in Europe and the United States, they are not homogenous. Indeed, their migration histories are different, with many Montenegrins

Table 3.2 Remittance Flows in Balkan Economies

	Remittance Inflow (Million USD)							
	2010	2011	2012	2013	2014	2015	2016	2017
Albania	1,519	1,552	1,420	1,282	1,421	1,291	1,306	1,382
BiH	1,822	1,958	1,846	1,958	2,107	1,801	1,846	2,010
Croatia	1,900	2,092	2,085	2,174	2,149	2,104	2,190	2,307
Kosovo	1,007	993	946	1,058	1,099	971	986	1,115
Macedonia	388	434	394	376	367	307	291	314
Montenegro	335	401	398	423	431	381	396	426
Serbia	4,118	3,960	3,549	4,025	3,696	3,371	3,205	3,588
Slovenia	347	489	253	309	369	423	364	406
Worldwide	467,503	524,904	545,604	576,407	597,859	582,053	573,131	613,466

moving to neighbouring Serbia where the impact of war was more benign. In B&H, many people moved internally within the country in order to escape conflict, and Kosovo saw people leave the small province and escape to other countries. Given the forced nature of this migration, the diaspora are difficult to properly identify, as they are scattered around the world and the majority do not have formal connections to the homeland.

Despite differences in demographic, conflict, and migration histories, the three economies of B&H, Kosovo, and Montenegro provide a useful comparison, having all experienced the fall of socialism, the break-up of the former Yugoslavia, conflict and violence which has led to the population displacements, and economic and demographic imbalances which have continued to creating outward migration and low growth (FMECD, 2012).

3.6. Conclusion

This chapter has set out the importance of institutions for fostering entrepreneurship. Institutional arrangements change over time, meaning that the prevailing frameworks can be supportive or indeed hinder entrepreneurship as they evolve. Policy makers can change the formal rules governing entrepreneurial activity, although informal institutions are slower to shift. If the culture remains averse to entrepreneurship, then formal institutional change will be less effective. Yet informal institutions are not 'unyielding obstacles' (Winiecki, 2001) and change is possible. Given that the returns to different forms of entrepreneurship are sensitive to institutional contexts (Estrin et al., 2016), it is only when change in institutions leads to higher rates of productive entrepreneurial activity that they will be regarded to have been a success.

Post-conflict economies have experienced path break in their institutions as their newborn status has required them to move away from the old institutional arrangements of the past and create new frameworks. Reforms to formal institutions have taken place. Yet unless entrepreneurs perceive the benefits of these reforms, more productive activity will not be harnessed. If entrepreneurs perceive stability and certainty, then formal institutional changes will become embedded. However, if entrepreneurs perceive change and uncertainty, they will either avoid activity which exposes them to risks or will seek to circumvent rules.

B&H, Kosovo, and Montenegro have created new institutional arrangements which seek to foster entrepreneurship and growth. Yet all three countries can still be characterised by weak institutions, with instability creating significant risks to entrepreneurial activity. This will clearly deter entrepreneurship at home, but will also impact the willingness of the diaspora to invest at home. Individuals can weigh the differential returns associated with entrepreneurship in their host and home countries. Returns to profit will differ between home and host country due to the institutional arrangements in place. As this book shows, this will not only impact the types of entrepreneurial activities that are invested in in the homeland, but also how they develop over time. Other forms of return, such as the returns to self associated with emotional attachment, may be a stronger motivating factor than profit.

Chapter 4 builds on the institutional analysis by examining how policy is seeking to engage returnee entrepreneurs through reform. It will show that much of the previous policy emphasis was on gaining remittances from the diaspora. However, such approaches have evolved, with a much greater emphasis on extracting wider benefits of entrepreneurial activity for the homeland.

4

Bringing the Diaspora Home

Policy Development and Priorities for Returnee
Investment

4.1. The Role of Policy

This chapter examines the development of policies which seek to mobilise
and maximise the potential of the diaspora to return home as entrepreneurs.
Through an analysis of relevant literature and policy documents in B&H,
Kosovo, and Montenegro, the chapter shows that these post-conflict economies are aiming to mobilise returnees in order to contribute to reconstruction and development. The chapter will show that while similar strategies are
being introduced in the three economies, they ways in which these are translated into coordinated policy differ. The translation of strategies into effective
policy is important if the diaspora is to be mobilised to contribute productively to economic development at home.

The majority of lower income countries have policies to welcome and encourage foreign investment, and often find themselves in competition for
such investment (Gillespie et al., 1999; Riddle and Brinkerhoff, 2011; Gamlen,
2014; Dickinson, 2017). This chapter focuses on one of these strategies, namely
the engagement of the diaspora for inward entrepreneurial investments,
which has become increasingly institutionalised within recent establishment
of ministries of diaspora affairs (Clemens et al., 2014). Following Sinatti and
Horst (2015), 'engagement' with returnees is defined as the initiatives set up in
pursuit of channelling investment and different forms of capital to the homeland. However, the chapter shows that diaspora engagement policy is often
uncoordinated, meaning that specific types of investment are not targeted.
Rather, the policy approach is that any type of investment is sought, above and
beyond what is already delivered through remittances.

In examining policy aimed at returnees in B&H, Kosovo, and Montenegro,
a framework is presented which shows that negative changes in a system stimulate responses and that the effects of these responses can return the system
to a 'norm' of economic growth (Figure 4.1). The model demonstrates that the

The Diaspora and Returnee Entrepreneurship. Nick Williams, Oxford University Press (2021). © Oxford University Press.
DOI: 10.1093/oso/9780190911874.003.0004

'norm' to be achieved by a system is a situation of economic growth where the response to positive and negative changes can bring about effects which help to create more resilient economies which are better able to withstand shocks (Simmie and Martin, 2009; Williams and Vorley, 2014). The framework shows the negative impact of the break-up of the former Yugoslavia, which created significant challenges for the newly independent states of B&H, Kosovo, and Montenegro. Already weak economies were made weaker still by the waves of migration during and after the wars, and policy makers face the challenge of returning to a 'norm' of economic stability, albeit one which improves on the previous economies when each nation was a province of Yugoslavia. Mobilising the diaspora has the potential to contribute to economic and social development and thus return the system towards the 'norm' of stability. In developing this framework, the chapter illustrates the role that the diaspora can play in fostering development in their country of origin, the necessity of engaging with the diaspora to improve economic outcomes, and also the challenge of creating the right policy mix to ensure that they are effectively mobilised.

4.2. Attracting Returnee Entrepreneurs Home

Targeting the diaspora to return and invest in their homeland has become popular amongst policy makers (Brinkerhoff, 2012). The emotional ties to their country of origin mean that they are often more willing to improve and contribute to the country's economic and social standing without a solely financial motive. Policy makers often view the diaspora as actual communities rooted in a national 'home' and sharing a group identity (Sinatti and Horst, 2015). As such, the diaspora are often targeted, as they have the potential for a large home country effect (Gillespie et al., 1999), and policy is also made imperative by weak institutional environments compared to more developed countries (Newland and Tanaka, 2010; Martinez et al., 2015).

Until recently, diaspora engagement activities have been typically uncoordinated (Gamlen, 2014), with governments in the country of origin targeting and interacting with the diaspora in direct and indirect ways. Indirect forms incorporate general improvements to the institutional environment in an economy. Navigating institutional frameworks is always challenging, but particularly so for diaspora entrepreneurs who may never have lived in the country of origin, have lived abroad for a number of years, or who know relatively few people in the country (Nielsen and Riddle, 2010). However, diaspora entrepreneurs are often the first foreign investors who move into uncertain political and economic climates (Gillespie et al., 2001) and as such, many countries are seeking creative ways to engage with and mobilise diaspora activity (Riddle et al., 2008).

In order to do this, direct forms of support have included policies specifically targeting the diaspora, typically in terms of finance and support, what Gamlen (2014) refers to as 'diaspora institutions', defined as offices of state dedicated to emigrants and their descendants. Yet engagement is multifaceted, and 'the state' is often not an easily identifiable set of institutions or policies, but a dispersed set of everyday practices that cohere in particular socio-temporal contexts into state-like effects, and thus provide scholars of diaspora policy with a more distributed conceptualisation of power and agency (Dickinson, 2017). Indeed, 'diaspora institutions' vary widely in form and function, from administrative departments, directorates, and other units, with some within the office of the president or prime minister, or within labour/employment ministries, as well as digital platforms for engagement, which are an attempt to map the diaspora and understand what activities they are willing to engage in more effectively (Brinkerhoff, 2009). Without such platforms, provision is often disparate (Ho, 2011). Within these institutions, a wide range of provision is often offered, with a popular approach being empowering diaspora agencies to develop and deliver policy (Federal Ministry for Economic Cooperation and Development, 2012). Empowering agencies is important in ensuring coordination of policy as well as cost-effectiveness. For example, in Chile the Office for Chileans Abroad is a department within the Ministry of Foreign Affairs responsible for providing services to the diaspora and facilitating their participation in economic development; while in Mexico, the Institute for Mexicans Abroad also sits within the Ministry of Foreign Affairs and has a large field presence through Mexico's consulates (Agunias and Newland, 2012). Such approaches are critical in ensuring a 'one-stop-shop' approach to providing advice and support to the diaspora as they act as the focal point for communication (Nielsen and Riddle, 2010). A further common approach is matching grants schemes, which can address one of the key barriers to diaspora investment, namely the financial risk associated with an unfavourable business environment. Projects are provided with funding on the condition that the recipient makes a specified contribution to the same project, and may assist in bringing in private investments into growing investments (Agunias and Newland, 2012). In Mexico, a 3 + 1 scheme was created, meaning that for every dollar raised by the diaspora for a specific project, each of the three levels of government (municipal, state, and federal) would match it dollar for dollar. A further common approach is the attraction of high-skilled workers from the diaspora with aim of ensuring the transfer of knowledge to those within the country of origin. The Migration for Development in Africa (MIDA) programmes have been implemented in a number of African countries and support the short, long, and virtual return of expatriates to a country's priority sector (Newland and Tanaka, 2010). The Transfer of Knowledge Through Expatriate Nationals (TOKTEN) programme covers travel expenses, daily allowances, and insurance of diaspora experts to engage in consulting opportunities in their country of origin (International Labour Organisation, 2001).[1] Similar to this, Germany has a returning experts programme which supports junior as well as experienced individuals from a list of lower income countries who have completed their education in Germany but would like to return to their country of origin (Agunias and Newland, 2012).

Improvements in institutions are clearly important for lower income economies, not simply for attracting more diaspora investment, but more generally to secure growth and slow down outward migration. In this regard, there has been some attempt to involve diaspora communities in the development of formal institutions (Riddle and Brinkerhoff, 2011; Kshetri, 2013), defined as the rules and regulations governing economic activity in a country (Williams and Vorley, 2015). Similarly, informal institutions, defined as the prevailing norms and values, have also been targeted in order to enhance absorptive capacity, for example through the use of diaspora networks for business advice and mentorship (Kshetri, 2013). Involving the diaspora in policy making can be beneficial as they have the potential to act as change agents in their country of origin (Riddle and Brinkerhoff, 2011), with diasporans considered as emerging agents of development (Weinar, 2010). Kshetri (2013) examined the influence of diaspora communities on implementing institutional changes across economies and political systems, and found 'top-down' approaches: China, with a strong state and weak civil society, imposed limitations on the political and social influences of diasporas; whereas India mobilised their diaspora through religious, social, economic, and political associations and these gave rise to enhanced economic opportunities. Given the variety of approaches used, and different levels of engagement with the diaspora, it is important to examine the effectiveness of policy (Gamlen, 2014).

The three economies of B&H, Kosovo, and Montenegro provide a useful lens for comparing policy making, having all experienced the fall of socialism,

---

[1] The Transfer of Knowledge Through Expatriate Nationals (TOKTEN) was initially established by the United Nations Development Programme (UNDP) in 1976 as one of the earliest cultural initiatives to encourage migrants to contribute their expertise for the benefit of their country of origin, and aims to counter the effects of the 'brain drain' by matching migrants with appropriate expertise for short-term consultancy assignments in their country of origin.

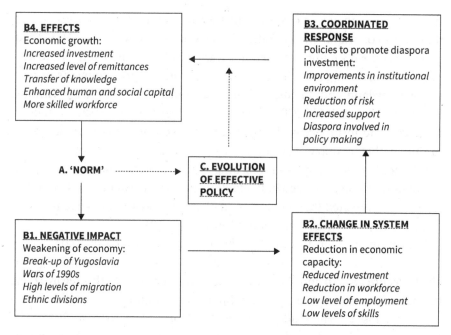

Figure 4.1   Feedback loops created by shock, outward migration, and policy response.
Source: Williams (2018).

the break-up of the former Yugoslavia, conflict and violence which have led to population displacements, and economic and demographic imbalances which have continued to create outward migration and low growth (Federal Ministry for Economic Cooperation and Development, 2012). The following section of the chapter examines the challenges of policies which seek to harness the economic potential of the diaspora communities in B&H, Kosovo, and Montenegro. It shows that policy attention on the diaspora has taken different forms in each of the three economies, and that obstacles to effectively mobilising the diaspora remain.

4.3. Policy in Post-Conflict Economies

In order to examine diaspora policy in the Balkan economies of B&H, Kosovo, and Montenegro, this chapter draws on a framework presented in Williams (2018) which sets out the benefits to the country of origin of mobilising diaspora communities, as well as the policy challenges (Figure 4.1). In the case of the Balkan economies, the break-up of Yugoslavia, the wars of the 1990s, and ongoing ethnic divisions created a negative impact on each of the economies

(B1). While they achieved independence, each country faced significant economic challenges, including ongoing migration of the skilled workforce. The negative effect caused a reduction in economic capacity, reduced investment, low levels of employment and skills, as well as a reduction in the overall workforce due to outward migration (B2). In response to this, part of the policy approach has been a coordinated response to mobilise the diaspora to create a positive impact on the economy (B3), with the aims being to better coordinate policy, reduce the risks associated with investment, increase support, improve the institutional environment, and involve the diaspora in policy making. Through the effective coordination and implementation of policy, governments are seeking to improve economic growth through increased investment and increased levels of remittances, the transfer of knowledge to the country of origin, enhancements in human and social capital, and a more skilled workforce (B4), all of which can be impacted by effective mobilisation of the diaspora, and return the economies to the 'norm' of positive growth. Given the changing institutional environment, for example in response to external pressures or changes in government priorities, a smooth path of reform and progress cannot be guaranteed; rather, the economies will fluctuate positively and negatively as policy takes shape and has an impact. However, with commitment to effective policies over time (C), economies can bypass or at least minimise shocks to the system so that beneficial impacts are secured.

4.3.1. Policy Approaches in Bosnia and Herzegovina, Kosovo, and Montenegro

The literature review demonstrates that policy approaches to mobilising the diaspora are multifaceted and often uncoordinated and ill-defined (Gamlen, 2014). Previously, policy aimed at the diaspora has been criticised for being centred on 'extracting obligations', asking 'what the diaspora can do for them' rather than what they can do for diaspora investors (Gamlen, 2006). In addition, developing diaspora institutional changes is particularly challenging in post-conflict economies, where government emphasis is on building nascent and fragile institutional environments, and where coordination between different departments and levels of government is often lacking (Nielsen and Riddle, 2010).

However, over time, the role of the diaspora and how they can be engaged has evolved. They have come to be a key part of economic and social policy in many lower income economies (Riddle and Brinkerhoff, 2011). In B&H, Kosovo, and Montenegro, governments are seeking to better coordinate policy so that greater benefits can be accrued from mobilising the diaspora. Table 4.1 draws on a literature review of diaspora policy to show common approaches and the diaspora need or challenge the policies are seeking to address. It also shows how policy has developed in B&H, Kosovo, and Montenegro and emphasises the disparate nature of provision, with central provision often lacking, while attempts to broker relationships, impact perceptions, and enhance emotional ties remain underdeveloped. Table 4.1 also demonstrates how the background institutional environments have been slow to develop in each of the three countries, meaning that investment has been stymied.

Each of the B&H, Kosovar, and Montenegrin governments emphasises the importance of the diaspora for development. Policy is most coordinated in Montenegro, which has a Directorate for Diaspora falling under the Ministry of Foreign Affairs, and there is a Strategy of Cooperation with Diaspora and a Strategy for Integrated Migration Management in Montenegro; however, these have yet to be adopted as policy (Federal Ministry for Economic Cooperation and Development, 2012; Government of Montenegro, 2014). Despite this, Montenegro has had a number of disparate policy approaches. The Register of Montenegro's Diaspora represented an organised way of communication with the Montenegrin Diaspora, and the Montenegro Diaspora Centre was established in 2002 as an independent governmental body with the purpose of being the bridge for cooperation of Montenegrin emigrants from all over the world with their home country (European Commission, 2012). The Montenegro Diaspora Centre, which operates within the Ministry of Foreign Affairs, is the main institution coordinating and promoting diaspora links with their homeland. The Centre provides support in the organisation of visits of business, cultural, and other delegations from emigrant destination countries to Montenegro, and also developed a Fund for Diaspora, which consists in offering loans to help diaspora members start a small or medium-size business. However, this programme has not yet been implemented, and the Centre has had between 5 and 10 members of staff and a budget equivalent to 0.05% of the national budget (Government of Montenegro, 2014) and as such is unlikely to produce substantial impacts. The Montenegrin government states that emigration trends mean that more needs to be done to engage members of the country's diaspora and that managing this human and intellectual potential is an essential condition for further progress and development of Montenegro (Ministry of Foreign Affairs, 2012). Translating this policy emphasis into effective action is conditional on government ministries and partner organisations working together.

The lack of policy coordination is even more pronounced in B&H and Kosovo, in part due to the ethnic divisions which are still evident in politics

Table 4.1 Government Policy in Strengthening Diaspora Investment and Entrepreneurship

Government Role	Diaspora Need/Challenge	Case Study Policies		
		B&H	Kosovo	Montenegro
Central focus of policy and support	Requirement of political support and political commitment to diaspora over time	No ministry; provision fragmented	Dedicated Ministry of the Diaspora; yet policy slow to develop	No ministry, but Directorate for Diaspora; lack of political commitment and administrative capacity
Provision of information	Lack of information regarding investment opportunities; difficulties navigating institutional challenges	Inconsistency of information between Federation and Republika Srpska	Establishment of digital network	Register of Montenegro's Diaspora and Montenegro Diaspora Centre; although both have limited resources
Brokering relationships	Difficulties identifying suitable contacts to assist with entrepreneurial development	Previously involved in TOKTEN scheme; Re-connect Scheme to engage in economic activity	Homeland Engagement Programme to allow short-term deployment of diaspora experts proposed but not operational; to become part of Expert Return Programme run by German government	Register of Montenegro's Diaspora to enhance networks
Impacting perceptions	Concerns about risks associated with investment; fears regarding property and other legal rights	Institutional reforms to encourage investment have been slow; negative perceptions of risk still common	Institutional reforms to encourage investment have been slow; policy emphasises that diaspora have been seen as emergency financial 'lifeline' with little done to impact long-term perceptions	Institutional reforms to encourage investment have been slow; negative perceptions of risk common although improving
Enhancing emotional ties	Lack of feeling of belonging (especially second generation)	Party of the Bosnia and Herzegovina Diaspora to engage diasporans in political process	Plans to involve diasporans in political process; motivation to invest as protest against (previous) Serbian rule and now Serbian opposition to independence	Council for Cooperation with Diaspora Members to promote links to the homeland

Source: Williams (2018).

and geography with regards to majority Bosniak (Bosnia Federation) and majority Serb (Republika Srpska) areas in Bosnia, and majority Albanian and majority Serb parts of the country in Kosovo, and which make policy coordination at the national level extremely challenging. While B&H does not have a dedicated policy for diaspora engagement at present, the Strategy on Migration and Asylum of Bosnia and Herzegovina and its Action Plan 2016–2020 focus on strengthening the institutional and policy frameworks for the purpose of linking diaspora and economic development (Ministry of Security, 2016). The Action Plan recognises the vast potential of mobilising the diaspora for development in B&H in terms of human, economic, and social potential, and the willingness of migrants to help their home country. B&H is divided on ethnic lines, with diaspora policy falling under the Ministries of Displaced Persons and Refugees in the Federation, while in Republika Srpska there is less policy coordination focused on mobilising the diaspora (MHRR, 2016). In both parts of the country, the prevailing institutions can be a driving force for diaspora engagement, yet 'could also be a restraining factor if they fail to engage in the country-wide policy vision setting in this area or promote all-inclusive outreach to diaspora regardless of their ethnicity' (MHRR, 2016, p. 9).

The Government of Kosovo launched a Ministry of Diaspora in 2011, which is unique among the three economies studied, but which previously existed in Serbia before being merged into the Ministry of Culture. The Ministry is responsible for coordinating efforts to work with diaspora abroad and harness their investment and involvement at home (Government of Kosovo, 2015). Despite this, no legislation has been passed to bring in direct policies to mobilise the diaspora; rather, the Ministry is trying to coordinate a range of existing, disparate, and small-scale activities across the country. Within these attempts, Kosovo has also started work on a National Development Strategy (NDS) which has the strategic vision to secure the economic development of the country up to 2020, and to secure social cohesion and inclusion, and within which are policies and strategies to mobilise the activities of the diaspora to benefit the economy (Government of Kosovo, 2016). In addition, the Strategy for Diaspora 2014–2017 is a key guiding policy, which sets out the goals of supporting diaspora integration in their host countries while at the same time preserving their cultural identity and facilitating investments and transfer of skills to their home country (Office of the Prime Minister, 2016). There is, however, no evidence that this strategy has led to any actual changes in policy as yet. Previously, diaspora communities in Kosovo were motivated to invest in part as a reaction against Serbian rule (Office of the Prime Minister, 2016). With independence from Serbia, Kosovo still experiences ethnic divisions, especially in the north of the country, which is majority Serb, and political challenges associated with inclusivity remain. This means that diaspora investment is 'highly fragmented along political and ideological lines' (Office of the Prime Minister, 2016, p. 10).

In addition to the complex governance arrangements in B&H and Kosovo, and more unified arrangements in Montenegro, economic and social policy in the three economies is also influenced by EU accession ambitions. As Montenegro is an official candidate for EU accession, while B&H and Kosovo have EU accession as explicit elements of their foreign policy while not being official candidates, this could be expected to have an impact on diaspora policy. B&H's Reform Agenda 2015–2018 confirms the EU accession trajectory of policy, and has incorporated the submission of a formal application for launching negotiations with the European Union (Efendic et al., 2014). Kosovo's NDS is also explicit about policy being in harmony with EU integration processes, although it is non-specific about what this means in practice for diaspora policy. In Montenegro, a more explicit EU influence on policy is found. From 2008, Montenegro has had access to the Instrument for Pre-Accession Assistance and has received over €300 million in funding, making it the country with the largest European aid per citizen in the Western Balkan region (European Commission, 2012). Despite this, the 'Indicative Strategy Paper' which sets out the European Union's accession requirements makes no mention of the role of diaspora communities, and only discusses migration in the context of inflows to the country (European Commission, 2014). As such, notwithstanding significant external involvement in economic and social policy making in the Balkans following the break-up of the former Yugoslavia (Xheneti et al., 2013), this has not filtered down into diaspora policy, despite its potential to have a significant impact on development, and the fact that many of the Balkan diaspora reside in EU countries.

4.3.2. Improving the Institutional Environment

As is clear, there is a lack of policy coordination in B&H, Kosovo, and Montenegro which will undermine efforts to mobilise the diaspora. However, there have been significant changes in the institutional frameworks of each economy. The three countries have experienced major disruption to their political and economic landscapes following the wars and break-up of Yugoslavia, akin to what Acemoglu and Robinson (2012) describe as 'critical junctures' in development. Despite the numerous challenges, this has created the opportunity for positive reforms, with ensuring the rule of law (Estrin et al., 2016), as well as the expectations that institutions are stable to ensure legitimacy and compliance (Crawford and Ostrom, 1995) of critical importance, especially in post-conflict environments (Nielsen and Riddle, 2010).

In post-conflict economies the environment for doing business can be adverse and is typically characterised by weak formal institutions and poor enforcement of laws, regulations, and property rights (Hoxha, 2009; Nielsen and Riddle, 2010; Welter and Smallbone, 2011). In situations where the diaspora view the institutional environment as challenging, for example through exhibiting political instability, corruption, and weak legal protection, investment will be discouraged (Kosmo and Nedelkoska, 2015). The economies of B&H, Kosovo, and Montenegro face similar challenges to transition economies, as they have moved from a centrally planned economic system under the former Yugoslavia to a market-based economy, which has meant a changing environment for economic activity (Vorley and Williams, 2016b). Yet, as discussed in Chapter 3, these economies are in many ways distinct from transition economies, as they have been required to create institutions that did not exist previously at the national level of B&H, Kosovo, and Montenegro. The institutions of the former Yugoslavia have not been transferred to the newborn states as they have sought to move away from centrally planned economies and associations with the political past. This has provided an impetus for reform, with much economic development policy implanted from Western economies with little consideration of local conditions (Williams and Vorley, 2017). In addition, the conflicts created considerable outward migration which policy makers have responded to with a range of policies designed to encourage investment in the homeland.

In B&H, Kosovo, and Montenegro, diaspora investment is stymied by institutional challenges, particularly the financial risks to investment, poor flow of information and facilitation of services, mistrust in the country's institutions, and the collective action problem caused by political fragmentation (MHRR, 2016; Office of the Prime Minister, 2016). Only one of the three countries (Kosovo) has a ministry dedicated to diaspora support and engagement. In B&H and Montenegro there is no central department with overall control of policy, and governance is often split along ethnic divides. Even Montenegro, which has the simplest form of governance, is described as having a 'lack of administrative capacity and fragmentation . . . [which] impedes policy at times' (Government of Montenegro, 2014, p. 14).

The countries' key policy documents highlight that institutional arrangements are ineffective and need to be redesigned through centralised services as well as specific support programmes. While much of the institutional development in each of the countries is not specific to attracting diaspora investment, as the focus in post-conflict environments is often on improving the general institutional framework (Nielsen and Riddle, 2010), there have been diaspora-specific institutional changes in each economy. The policy documents make clear that the critical aspects of these are the extension of support services and communication of what is available to the diaspora (MHRR, 2016; Office of the Prime Minister, 2016). Diaspora-specific programmes demonstrate that activities are taking place, albeit in a piecemeal and highly dispersed way. B&H took part in the TOKTEN scheme, which received a great deal of government exposure as part of efforts to encourage highly qualified members of the diaspora living abroad to undertake short-term consultancy contracts in their home country, and in total 32 consultants worked with local institutions (Efendic et al., 2014). In addition, B&H has had the Re-Connect scheme, which involved the transfer of knowledge and skills from young B&H diaspora to re-engage with their native country and to help the country's development. Other programmes include Domestic Product Promotion Alliance, a programme in which members of the diaspora are required to invest in production in B&H and to support national companies to compete more successfully in international markets; B&H Students, which involves the exchange of ideas and information flows between students inside and outside the country; Reconstruction, Capacity Building and Development through the return of qualified nationals; and the Temporary Return of Qualified Nationals (Efendic et al., 2014). At present, despite the Ministry for Diaspora and NDS, Kosovo has no central, coordinated approach to mobilising the diaspora; however, it does have a number of planned activities as part of its strategic vision. These include the organisation of regular diaspora business fairs, conferences, and forums; agreements with diaspora host countries on issues such as avoidance of double taxation, protection of investments, and issuance of investment guarantees by the Kosovo government; the provision of tax breaks and other financial incentives on imports; and the establishment of a digital network, which it is hoped will assist in mapping the locations of the diaspora and understanding their motivations more clearly (Government of Kosovo, 2015, 2016). In addition, there are strategic plans to induce more diaspora investments, including an International Guarantee Fund, Private Investment Fund, Diaspora Banking Products, Economic Zones, and Municipal Bonds, although some of these are planned to operate at a municipal level rather than nationally (Office of the Prime Minister, 2016). The NDS specifies how new 'concrete activities' are required to ensure that the impact of the diaspora is maximised (Government of Kosovo, 2016, p. 16). Similar to Montenegro's Register of Montenegro's Diaspora, the NDS states that a database needs to be established to provide a central contact point to engage with the diaspora; that a Homeland Engagement Programme should be established which will allow the short-term deployment of diaspora experts and students in public, educational, and private companies through subsidies; and that a TOKTEN scheme needs to be established (Government of Kosovo, 2016). In addition, Kosovo will become part of the Expert Return Programme introduced by the German government, which will allow short-term deployment of diaspora experts in Kosovo (Government of Kosovo, 2016).

The lack of central coordination of diaspora policy and intervention does not mean that support is entirely absent. In fact, support does exist but is disparate, with different localities offering support, for example through Chambers of Commerce, Councils, or non-governmental organisations (Federal Ministry for Economic Cooperation and Development, 2012). The disparate nature of interactions is emphasised in Kosovo's NDS, which states that there is a need for a transition from the diaspora's role as a 'traditional and spontaneous role as an emergency financial lifeline', a role in which they feel 'increasingly frustrated and even abused', to one where 'its resources are used more strategically for long-term development purposes' (Office of the Prime Minister, 2016, p. 7). There are numerous connections at the local level through homeland villages' links to the diaspora abroad (Federal Ministry for Economic Cooperation and Development, 2012), yet engagement in such disparate provision will be mixed, with diaspora members often relying on philanthropic intermediaries to channel donations to specific community projects in their home country or giving directly to family and friends (Agunias and Newland, 2012). Furthermore, the uncoordinated nature of support impacts diaspora perceptions of the 'readiness' of economies to engage in their expertise and foster investment (Kosmo and Nedelkoska, 2015), and will thus undermine the willingness of the diaspora to invest in their home country (Gillespie et al., 1999). In order to overcome these barriers, each of the main policy documents in B&H, Kosovo, and Montenegro communicate the importance of 'one-stop shops', providing the diaspora with a centralised and visible focus for accessing support and channelling investments. Yet despite this emphasis, potential diaspora investors often need more than just the access to market and operational information that such provision offers. As Nielsen and Riddle (2010) note, they need trustworthy, reliable contacts, including key government officials, bankers, buyers, suppliers, distributors, management and tax consultants, and individuals and organisations who can assist the diaspora with her/his human resource management, marketing, and legal needs. As such, one-stop shops are often insufficient in mobilising investment.

The analysis of policy reports demonstrates how institutional environments in the three economies of B&H, Kosovo, and Montenegro have changed considerably since independence, and that diaspora policies are being foregrounded as part of formal institutional changes. This is of critical importance in persuading the diaspora that stable environments exist in each country, which minimises risk, so that the perceptions improve and thus investment is encouraged.

4.3.3. The Transfer of Knowledge to Entrepreneurs and Policy Makers

The disparate nature of current policy activity means that a crucial benefit of diaspora investment, the transfer of knowledge, is not being adequately harnessed. The policy initiatives demonstrate that a key aim of attempts to mobilise the diaspora is for the home country to benefit from transfers of knowledge. Diaspora investment leads to transfers of knowledge which can impact working practices and entrepreneurial activity in the country of origin (Riddle et al., 2010; Levin and Barnard, 2013; World Bank, 2016). Cultural knowledge can place the diaspora at an advantage in terms of investment opportunities (Vershinina et al., 2011). In addition, it can lead to enhancements in human and social capital, and improvements in skills, among the population in the country of origin working with or receiving remittances from the diaspora. Moreover, the transfer of knowledge can also directly influence policy making, allowing governments to make better decisions about how to effectively engage the diaspora.

In Montenegro, government intervention is underdeveloped in terms of transfer of knowledge to policy makers. The policy focus with regards to transfers has been on promoting higher levels, and more efficient administration, of remittances (European Commission, 2012). While important, improvements in this area lie mainly in the hands of financial institutions and transfer agencies in the private sector and have not led to enhancement of policy. Effective engagement with the diaspora to inform policy has been absent. However, the government has recently established a Council for Cooperation with Diaspora Members, which has been passed into law (Government of Montenegro, 2016). The Council is made of 77 members, representing various different institutions from government departments, municipalities, embassies, Chambers of Commerce, and representative organisations from different ethnic groups. The Council will aim to cooperate more effectively with the diaspora, partly through securing their involvement in an intergovernmental commission for economic cooperation, as well as arranging various local-level support activities and awareness-raising of opportunities. While the impacts of the Council remain to be seen, it does represent a step forward in involving diaspora in policy making, and should ensure that the ineffective implementation of previous cooperative measures (European Commission, 2012) is, at least partly, overcome.

In B&H, government agencies have struggled to engage the diaspora in policy making. As such, they have not stimulated the diaspora's sense of belonging and connectivity (MHRR, 2016). This is despite the implementation of the TOKTEN programme, which, while recognised as an effective policy lever (International Labour Organisation, 2001), did not create wider and more lasting transfers of knowledge. Indeed, policy documents demonstrate that there is a lack of institutional capacity for more active diaspora engagement in government decision-making, which is 'primarily reflection of the complex administrative, economic and political environment in B&H, further challenged with a lack of institutional cooperation, and a consequent lack of knowledge about the relationship between diaspora and development' (Efendic et al., 2014). Similarly, Kosovo's NDS states that there are currently no mechanisms to ensure diaspora involvement in decision-making, as the diaspora has 'no voice in government' and 'policies too strongly driven by governments can act as a deterrent for diaspora engagement' (Office of the Prime Minister, 2016, p. 11). This reduces the diaspora's trust in policy making and, given that a sense of belonging is important to securing diaspora investment (Nielsen and Riddle, 2010), means that it will not be mobilised. The NDS is clear that there are 'no specific plans in place' to address this issue and notes that developments in this are 'largely dependent on high-level political processes, such as coalition agreements, in which political considerations play a greater role than strategic policy ones' (Office of the Prime Minister, 2016, p. 12). In common with other countries that have courted the diaspora through voting rights (Gamlen et al., 2017), there are plans to increase the voice of the diaspora by creating opportunities for it to vote abroad, as integration can lead to policy being more informed (De Haas, 2010). This, though, would only have a small and relatively insignificant influence on diaspora-related policy. B&H has a 'Party of the Bosnia and Herzegovina Diaspora', which states its aim to politically organise the diaspora and to contribute to the development of the country, and is making efforts to ensure the right to vote for returnees, internally displaced persons, and the diaspora in their places of pre-war residence (Efendic et al., 2014). However, the party's influence is small, having failed to win any national seats, and did not participate in local elections.

The importance of transfer of knowledge demonstrates how the impacts of diaspora on their home country are multifaceted. Diaspora policy is not narrowly focused on securing higher levels of remittances or the return home of skilled workers and entrepreneurs. Rather, it is seeking to involve the diaspora in a wide range of economic and social interventions, and part of the strategy for doing so is to involve them in decision-making. As diaspora communities have the potential to act as change agents in their country of origin (Riddle and Brinkerhoff, 2011), involving them in decision-making can lead to institutional improvements as it generates trust and ownership (Agunias and Newland, 2012), which in turn can trigger a demonstration effect which positively influences the economic activity of other diaspora members as well as individuals within the home country.

4.4. Conclusion

This chapter has examined the development of policies which seek to mobilise the potential of diaspora investment in their home countries. The framework presented in Figure 4.1 demonstrates how policy makers in post-conflict economies are faced with the challenge of mobilising diaspora as a result of shocks to their economy which have increased outward migration and undermined growth. In the case of the Balkan economies, this shock was created by the break-up of the former Yugoslavia, the wars of the 1990s and their legacy, and challenges associated with independent national status, all of which have created ongoing outward migration which has reduced economic capacity. Different shocks will create negative impacts in other economies, yet the challenges of mobilising the diaspora remain the same.

The analysis shows that mobilising the diaspora is a central strategic priority for economic development in each of the economies, in part due to the influence of EU policy requirements, but also in response to acute economic and demographic challenges in each of the economies. Despite this, strategic vision has not translated into policy practice, and as such the potential importance of the diaspora to B&H, Kosovo, and Montenegro is currently underdeveloped and characterised by a lack of coordination, in part due to ongoing political fragmentation. In one sense, this is understandable given the wide range of economic and social challenges policy makers have had to tackle in these post-conflict, newborn environments. Yet all three countries are currently aiming to develop more coherent and coordinated diaspora policies.

In many ways, policy coordination is simpler in Montenegro, as it has a less complex system of governance and less ethnic division. The divide between

Republika Srpska and the Bosniak Federation in Bosnia, and the majority Albanian and majority Serb areas of Kosovo, means that coordination is hampered by inter-governmental and inter-departmental challenges. Yet the analysis shows that even in Montenegro, where policy is relatively more coordinated, the potential impacts of diaspora engagement are being undermined by a lack of resources devoted to support and facilitation.

The disparate nature of provision which currently exists means that the mobilisation of diaspora investment is not being maximised. While the flow of remittances, which play a significant role in the economies of the Balkans, demonstrates that diaspora connections are in place, the spillover effect produced by the transfer of knowledge (Riddle and Brinkerhoff, 2011) is not being adequately harnessed. Individual family members who receive remittances benefit, and this may be utilised for economic activity, but the impact is highly localised. Centralised approaches to policy can help to ensure not only that the transfer of knowledge is maximised for all the individuals involved (both the diaspora and those receiving investment), but also that the knowledge from this can be shared and put into practice in other contexts. Crucially, there needs to be greater involvement of the diaspora in policy decision-making in B&H, Kosovo, and Montenegro. At present, while governments in the three countries are eager to improve their relationship with the diaspora, there is a lack of real engagement and consultation around policy making, meaning that participation and shaping of the policy agenda, which can be important in mobilising the diaspora (De Haas, 2010), is not occurring. The transfer of knowledge from diaspora to policy makers is not currently effective, and this is emphasised by the slow development of policy in each of the economies studied. While Montenegro's Council for Cooperation with Diaspora Members represents a step forward, its success remains to be seen; while in B&H and Kosovo there are no effective mechanisms for involving the diaspora and engendering ownership and trust. Schemes such as TOKTEN have some value, and provide a guide to policy makers for implementation, but need to be further embedded and extended given their focus on short-term engagement, if they are to have wider impact. Akin to other areas of public policy, such as entrepreneurship and economic development, the Balkan economies can seek to adopt policy from elsewhere and transfer it to a new context (Xheneti and Kitching, 2011). Programmes such as TOKTEN can be replicated and learnt from, and the application of this learning will enhance attempts to mobilise the diaspora; however, policy makers in B&H, Kosovo, and Montenegro need to do much more to learn from successful implementation, especially in their neighbouring countries.

The next chapter focuses on the strategic responses of returnee entrepreneurs when faced with challenging institutional environments. It shows that despite the good intentions of policy makers, their investment decisions will be largely influenced by how much trust they have in the reforms being made. As stated in Chapter 3, institutional reform is not linear and proceeds in a number of steps which influence the development of both formal rules and regulations, and also the informal norms and values within a country. As such, returnee entrepreneurs have to consider and navigate a changing institutional environment when making investment decisions, with these decisions determining the potential impact of investments on economic and social development.

5

Intention to Return

The Responses of Returnees to Home Institutional Environments

5.1. Entrepreneurial Intentions and Post-Conflict Economies

This chapter examines the intentions of the diaspora to return to their homeland and engage in entrepreneurial activity, with a focus on post-conflict economies where the development and reconstruction potential of the diaspora is significant. The chapter demonstrates that the entrepreneurial intentions of returning entrepreneurs are affected by their perceptions of risk in institutions at home. Through a survey of returnee entrepreneurs to Kosovo, the chapter finds that business experience has a negative relationship on probability to return, but it has a positive relationship on entrepreneurial intentions. However, those with professional and qualified jobs are more likely to have intentions to return, but are less likely to have entrepreneurial intentions. Implications for reconstruction and contributions to scholarship on returning diaspora entrepreneurship in post-conflict economies are discussed.

Given their international experience, returnee entrepreneurs are able to compare the institutional environments of their host country (i.e. the country they migrated to) to their home country (i.e. the country they migrated from). Post-conflict economies are often characterised by weak and underdeveloped institutional environments (Desai et al., 2013; Williams and Vorley, 2017). As such, perceptions of entrepreneurial opportunity at home will be weakened. This has implications for reconstruction and development, as diaspora entrepreneurs are able to contribute to the homeland in a number of ways. First, they can be involved in the direct involvement in the creation of new firms or the management of existing firms; second, they can invest in the entrepreneurial activities of others; and, third, they can act as role models to entrepreneurs in the home country and for non-diaspora foreign investors (Nielsen and Riddle, 2010). The 'demonstration effect' created by

The Diaspora and Returnee Entrepreneurship. Nick Williams, Oxford University Press (2021). © Oxford University Press.
DOI: 10.1093/oso/9780190911874.003.0005

entrepreneurial activity of the diaspora can be powerful in economies with low levels of entrepreneurship (Riddle et al., 2010).

As returns to different forms of entrepreneurial activity are sensitive to institutional contexts (Hashi and Krasniqi, 2010; Estrin et al., 2016), these contexts not only impact entrepreneurial activity in the home country, but also influence the willingness of entrepreneurs outside the country to invest (Riddle, Hrivnak, and Nielsen, 2010). Indeed, the institutional environment in post-conflict economies may prove daunting for even experienced diaspora since the environment is dynamic and marred by institutional deficiencies (Nielsen and Riddle, 2010). This can also lead to negative perceptions among diaspora communities who view the financial risk to investments, lack of support, political fragmentation and weak institutional framework as barriers to investment (Agunias and Newland, 2012). Changing such perceptions is an important element of institution building if higher levels of diaspora entrepreneurial activity are to be secured. As such, the chapter examines the role that institutional trust plays in driving or preventing diaspora entrepreneurship in post-conflict economies. Answering this question is important in understanding the potential for entrepreneurship to contribute to post-conflict reconstruction and development.

The chapter focuses on Kosovo and analyses data of returning diaspora individuals immediately after the country declared independence. The analysis finds that business experience has a negative relationship on probability to return; however, those with professional and qualified jobs are more likely to have intentions to return, but are less likely to have entrepreneurial intentions (Krasniqi and Williams, 2018). Harnessing the entrepreneurial intentions of the diaspora represents a key method for future development as post-conflict economies seek growth.

5.2. Analysing the Diaspora's Entrepreneurial Intentions

The chapter focuses on the case of Kosovo, and uses Riinvest Migrant's Survey data.[1] The data are based on a large survey of 715 migrants and contains detailed information about the individual characteristics (e.g. gender, age, education, occupation status, income [if working], and migration history), household characteristics (e.g. household size, marital status, and share of employed family members). The survey included interviews with migrants

---

[1] For more information on the survey, see Krasniqi and Williams (2018).

in many crossing points of Kosovo's borders (Prishtina International Airport, Hani i Elezit, Merdare, Porti i Durrsit in Albania, Gjilan). Multiple border locations were chosen for better coverage of the population of interest, as suggested by McKenzie and Mistiaen (2009). These multiple border crossing points are the main entrance routes to Kosovo for more than 90% of migrants.

The survey question 'Are you planning to return to Kosovo in the future?' differentiates between migrants with return and non-return intentions. The survey also differentiates between those with entrepreneurial intentions (through the question 'I feel confident to start up my business in Kosovo') only if they have plans to return to Kosovo. Of the total sample of migrants (715), 343 (48%) have return intentions, while 42 of them (nearly 6%) feel confident that they will start up their own business.

Two estimated probit regressions are presented in Table 5.1 and show that the main difference between the two equations is that we included family size, accumulated knowledge, experience during migration, and professional and qualified jobs. The two models show a high degree of self-selection among migrants. The instrumental variables 'Owns property in migration country' and 'Foreign origin spouse' both show a statistically significant negative relationship with return intention. These two variables were critical in the identification of equations. Existing literature suggests that marital status is a good instrument and can impact whether an individual stays or returns, but should not affect whether an individual becomes an entrepreneur (Hamdouch and Wahba, 2015).

From the personal characteristics of migrants, only variable age is statistically significant, suggesting a U-shaped relationship with return intentions, while it has a negative and statistically significant relationship with entrepreneurial intention. Following Hamdouch and Wahba (2015), migration duration can be used as a proxy for savings accumulation, suggesting that the longer the duration of stay in the host country, the higher the expected accumulated diaspora savings. Indeed, higher salaries, which are linked with age (experience and qualified jobs), may well decrease optimal migration durations (see Dustmann and Kirchkamp, 2002), having a positive impact on probability to return. However, we did not find evidence that optimal duration, which may signal higher savings, leads to higher potential for entrepreneurship intentions. However, as Kveder and Flahaux (2013) suggest, self-employment is not necessarily associated with positive migration experiences and well-paid jobs. The evidence suggests a U-shaped relationship between age and return, suggesting that the diaspora need time to accumulate some savings in order to return. In terms of entrepreneurship intentions, rather than a choice, self-employment appears to be a 'last resort' for individuals who were not

Table 5.1 Heckman Probit Model with Sample Selection for Migrant's Entrepreneurial Intention

Variables	(Model 1)		(Model 2)	
	Main Equation	Selection Equation	Main Equation	Selection Equation
Gender (male = 1)	−0.0477	0.0649	−0.0861	0.0183
	(0.215)	(0.145)	(0.163)	(0.151)
Migrant's age	−0.00495	−0.0552	0.0561	−0.0884**
	(0.0572)	(0.0369)	(0.0402)	(0.0381)
Migrant's age squared	−0.000136	0.000784*	−0.000827*	0.00114**
	(0.000655)	(0.000446)	(0.000477)	(0.000468)
Migration duration (years)	0.0375**	0.0194**	0.00224	0.00397
	(0.0155)	(0.00952)	(0.0114)	(0.0108)
Marital status (Married = 1)	−0.215	−0.0728	0.129	−0.115
	(0.233)	(0.138)	(0.163)	(0.150)
Employed family members	−0.00103	0.000169		
	(0.00600)	(0.000895)		
Self-employment experience abroad	0.117	0.0337	0.361*	−0.325*
	(0.293)	(0.179)	(0.192)	(0.189)
Forced migration (Kosovo War, 1999 = 1)	0.247	0.0242	0.0624	0.00480
	(0.285)	(0.165)	(0.123)	(0.0974)
Lack of trust in institutions (1 = lack of trust and high risk to open bank account in Kosovo)	−1.355***	−0.00239	−0.842***	0.0930
	(0.133)	(0.129)	(0.184)	(0.171)
University education prior to migration	0.331	0.294*	−0.0321	0.137
	(0.266)	(0.165)	(0.129)	(0.130)
Owns property in migration country		−0.454***		−0.281
		(0.134)		(0.196)
Foreign spouse		0.114		−0.250**
		(0.146)		(0.0996)
Family size			−0.0602	0.0583
			(0.0393)	(0.0387)
Accumulated knowledge and experience in migration			0.000817***	−0.00106***
			(0.000143)	(0.000144)
Professional and qualified jobs			−0.363***	0.459***
			(0.121)	(0.108)

Continued

Table 5.1 *Continued*

Variables	(Model 1)		(Model 2)	
	Main Equation	Selection Equation	Main Equation	Selection Equation
Constant	−0.497	0.587	−0.0339	1.643**
	(1.089)	(0.717)	(0.771)	(0.734)
Diagnostics				
Likelihood ratio test of independent equations $p=0, x^2_{(1)}$	2.72*		6.35**	
Log likelihood	−573.5562		−529.508	
Censored observation	372		370	
Uncensored observation	343		342	

The dependent variable in main equation equals 1 if migrant has return intention and entrepreneurial intention. The dependent variable in selection equation equals 1 if migrant has return intention.

Standard errors in parentheses.

*** $p < 0.01$; ** $p < 0.05$; * $p < 0.1$

Source: Krasniqi and Williams (2018).

able to accumulate capital or prepare for their return. Indeed, we find that the more time individuals spent in host country, the less likely they were to have entrepreneurial intentions. We did not find any statistical effect of conflict-induced migration on either probability to return or probability of entrepreneurial intentions.

The importance of institutions on migrants' intention to return and engage in entrepreneurship was then tested. The variable measuring importance of lack of trust and high risk associated with institutions is statistically significant. The analysis finds that migrants who lack trust in institutions and have high risk perceptions are less likely to have entrepreneurial intentions, while we did not find any effect on probability to return. This suggests that the institutional context is a critical factor in facilitating diaspora entrepreneurial activity in their homeland. This is because navigating institutional frameworks is always challenging, but particularly so for the diaspora who may never have lived in the home country, or who know relatively few people in the country (Nielsen and Riddle, 2010), and in a context of frequent changes and weak institutions. Therefore, improving institutions will assist in reducing the risks associated with return and thus foster greater levels of investment (Gamlen, 2014).

Existing research has found that the human capital accumulation of migrants in the form of business experience and skills development plays an important role in upgrading the knowledge base of the diaspora (see, for example, Hamdouch and Wahba, 2015). The analysis shows that migration experience enhances the skills and knowledge of the diaspora, which enables them to become entrepreneurs. Skills, qualifications, and professional jobs increase the probability to return, but reduce the likelihood of having entrepreneurial intentions. The migrants who hold 'professional and qualified jobs' are more likely to have return intentions, but they are less likely to have entrepreneurial intentions. Migrants holding professional jobs are more likely to return, but their choice may be salaried work or not being economically active instead of an entrepreneurial career. This type of skilled return migration can be beneficial for the home countries, as returnees bring new skills and competences, increase overall human capital, and enhance productivity and employment (Zaiceva and Zimmermann, 2016). Encouraging this category of returnees will assist reconstruction and development in the home country, for example by increasing the supply of qualified labour, the lack of which poses a significant problem for the development of the private sector in Kosovo (Krasniqi and Williams, 2018). As the majority of the Kosovan diaspora are based in the European Union and the United States, this implies that the skills and productivity of these workers may be comparatively higher than workers in Kosovo and can thus make a significant contribution at home. In addition, recent evidence suggests that although the unemployment rate in Kosovo is very high (around 35%), the private sector states that the lack of skilled labour poses severe problems for the development of businesses, and consequently the demand for high-level jobs could mean that the labour market may not be able to absorb skilled returnees (World Bank, 2011).

Self-employment experience in the host country and accumulated experience in specific industries are both statistically significant, increasing the probability of entrepreneurial intentions. This suggests that the similarity of a returnee's industry or sector background may positively influence entrepreneurial intentions. This may have significant policy implications in terms of investigating the motives to encourage their return in order to boost entrepreneurship by migrants in the home country. Policy attention could thus be directed to those among the diaspora with previous self-employment experience in the host country.

Table 5.2 reports corresponding marginal probabilities of migrants having entrepreneurial intentions conditional upon having the intention to return. Keeping all variables constant, individuals who have the intention to return on average have 8.8% probability of having entrepreneurial

Table 5.2 Marginal Effects after Probit with Sample Selection

Variables	dy/dx	Std. Err.	z	P>|z|	[95%	C.I.]	X
Gender (male = 1)	−0.057	0.084	−0.670	0.500	−0.222	0.108	0.875
Migrant's age	−0.021	0.025	−0.830	0.405	−0.070	0.028	38.278
Migrant's age squared	0.000	0.000	0.630	0.532	0.000	0.001	1550.560
Migration duration (years)	0.005	0.008	0.610	0.542	−0.011	0.020	12.302
Marital status (Married = 1)	0.019	0.082	0.230	0.821	−0.142	0.180	0.803
Family size	−0.005	0.024	−0.220	0.828	−0.053	0.042	3.579
Self-employment experience abroad	0.056	0.099	0.570	0.571	−0.138	0.251	0.079
University education prior to migration	0.071	0.065	1.090	0.275	−0.056	0.198	0.100
Accumulated knowledge and experience in migration	0.000	0.000	−1.540	0.123	0.000	0.000	563.253
Professional and qualified jobs	0.058	0.071	0.820	0.412	−0.081	0.198	0.681
Forced migration (Kosovo War, 1999 = 1)	0.054	0.081	0.670	0.502	−0.104	0.212	0.091
Lack of trust and high risk perception in institutions (1 = lack of trust and high risk to open bank account in Kosovo)	−0.568	0.092	−6.190	0.000	−0.748	−0.388	0.906
Owns property in migration country	−0.099	0.026	−3.840	0.000	−0.150	−0.049	0.052
Foreign spouse	−0.110	0.025	−4.380	0.000	−0.159	−0.061	0.117

y = Pr(entrepreneurial intention = 1 | return intention = 1) (predict, pcond) = 0.08836286.

Key: dy/dx is for discrete change of dummy variable from 0 to 1; Std. Err.: standard error; z: standard deviation from mean; P[Z]: probability less than z; 95% and CI: confidence intervals; x: sample mean.

Source: Krasniqi and Williams (2018).

intentions. Conditional upon having return intentions and keeping all other variables in the model constant at their means or specified at 1 for dummies, the migrants with a lack of trust and high-risk perceptions have on average 56.79% probability of having entrepreneurial intentions. This emphasises the importance of institutions on changing entrepreneurial intentions of Kosovo's diaspora.

5.3. Conclusions

As Chapter 3 illustrated, overcoming a lack of trust is a key element in harnessing entrepreneurial intentions towards the homeland. Intentions are the first step in a typically long-term process of starting a new business (Krueger, 1993; Thompson, 2009). This will be magnified for those individuals working across borders, who can compare institutional environments between home and host countries.

Many potential investors are discouraged by unstable institutional environments. This is true for entrepreneurs living within the country's borders, but it is magnified for those who are living or have lived outside the country, as they are able to compare the relative stability of their host country to home. Improving institutions is important for securing economic development, and is a significant focus of government efforts in post-conflict economies. The institutional environment in post-conflict economies may prove daunting for even experienced and well-connected diaspora investors since the environment is changeable (Nielsen and Riddle, 2010). As such, reconstruction through diaspora investment will be stymied.

Over time, tackling perceptions of risk and trust in institutions is important if investment is to be secured, as negative perceptions dampen entrepreneurial intentions. The analysis demonstrates that intentions vary among the diaspora, with business experience having a negative relationship on the probability to return. Aiming to attract experienced diaspora entrepreneurs means that post-conflict environments are in competition with the often more stable institutional environments of the host country. However, there is a positive relationship between business experience and probability to have entrepreneurial intentions, meaning that this can be tapped to benefit entrepreneurship in the home country. At the same time, the analysis shows that those with professional and qualified jobs are more likely to have intentions to return, but are less likely to have entrepreneurial intentions. This contrasts with existing research on returnee entrepreneurs to fast-growing economies where international experience can act as an impetus to undertake entrepreneurship at home (Wright et al., 2008; Qin et al., 2017). International experience acts to temper the potential for entrepreneurial activity at home, reflecting how the knowledge gained is not directly replicable at home due to unstable institutions and different business practices. In addition, individuals owning property in their host country are less likely to return, while those with university-level education prior to migration are more likely to return but less likely to have entrepreneurial intentions. This again reflects how post-conflict environments struggle to absorb the benefits of diaspora experience to benefit homeland reconstruction.

6

How Emotional Ties Influence the Diaspora to Return

6.1. Emotional Ties and Return

This chapter examines how emotional ties influence the investment activities of returnee entrepreneurs. Drawing on interviews with returnee entrepreneurs operating in B&H, Kosovo, and Montenegro, the chapter shows that although they face numerous institutional barriers, emotional ties provide returnees with the motivation to overcome challenges. The chapter demonstrates how emotional ties combine with international experience and perceptions of the institutional environment at home to influence activities towards societal outcomes rather than profit maximisation. Emotional ties assist in overcoming uncertainty and the barriers associated with it, and are not 'atomistic' in the sense that they are shaped by individual preferences or behaviours (Doern and Goss, 2013); rather, they evolve over time and are influenced by the specific context in which the activity takes place.

As Chapter 2 demonstrated, returnee entrepreneurs are viewed as having significant international experience which they can utilise to benefit the development of entrepreneurial activities at home (Wright et al., 2008). They are often embedded within their host countries but maintain connections to networks within their homeland. As such, they can be embedded across borders, with different returns to entrepreneurship available in home and host countries. Given this, returnee entrepreneurs may not invest in their homeland in order to gain profits. Instead, their emotional attachment to home places an emphasis on returns to self. This means that they gain a sense of pride in their investment, which is a more powerful motivating factor than profit. An emotional attachment and desire to contribute to the homeland mean that strategic decisions are made which aim to maximise individual feelings of self-worth, for example by targeting investments at helping family and friends. This has an impact at the entry stage, as mode of entry can be identified to maximise feelings of pride, rather than entrepreneurs identifying an opportunity which allows them to draw on their international experience.

The Diaspora and Returnee Entrepreneurship. Nick Williams, Oxford University Press (2021). © Oxford University Press.
DOI: 10.1093/oso/9780190911874.003.0006

Strategic decisions regarding entry are made to direct investments towards family and friends. These investments may be outside of the international experience of the returnee entrepreneur, and are often small in scale. In this sense, returnee entrepreneurship in adverse environments challenges theories of rapid internationalisation. Instead, returnee entrepreneurs may proceed slowly and incrementally to support family and friends, rather than opportunities associated with profit. A desire for such gains may be particularly strong in post-conflict economies, where an altruistic desire to improve the home country is borne out of the problems of the past. Returnee entrepreneurs can be motivated to invest in unstable environments that other investors consider to contain too many risks (Nkongolo-Bakenda and Chrysostome, 2013). As such, they make strategic decisions which aim to maximise emotional satisfaction, rather than maximising profit.

The analysis examined the motivations of returnee entrepreneurs, in order to understand why they had chosen to invest in their homeland. Monetary and non-monetary motivations were identified, and illustrate the key elements of individual gains being sought by returnee entrepreneurs. Personal motivations, as well as a desire to assist the home country to develop, are important. Overall, an emotional attachment to the homeland provides a push to overcome the institutional challenges that are present. Returnee entrepreneurs seek different outcomes associated with activity, and use their international experience for social impact rather than profit. The chapter also demonstrates how family and ethnic ties are utilised to enable activity at home, with many using informal networks to gain advantages, while some others use formal business networks.

6.2. Why We Returned

6.2.1. Understanding Returnee Entrepreneur Motivations

Table 6.1 provides a profile of the participants in terms of age, gender, the year of departure and year of return to B&H, Kosovo, and Montenegro (to invest or to live), whether they are a permanent resident of their home country, their host country location, and whether they maintain investments in their host country. It also shows whether their key economic activities when living in the host country were entrepreneurial or working for someone else. Some of the respondents maintained business interests in their host country, with a

Table 6.1 Profile of Respondents

Respondent	Age	Gender	Key Sector of Activity in Kosovo/B&H/ Montenegro	Entrepreneur in Host Country?	Year of Departure	Year of Return	Permanent Residence in Kosovo/B&H/ Montenegro	Host Country	Maintain Investments in Host Country?
Kosovo									
K1	42	Male	Media	Yes	1998	2012	Yes	Belgium	Yes
K2	55	Male	Construction	No	1994	2011	Yes	United States	No
K3	32	Male	Manufacturing	Yes	1996	2014	No	Germany	Yes
K4	45	Female	IT	No	1996	2014	Yes	United Kingdom	Yes
K5	58	Male	Financial services	No	1993	2010	No	Germany	Yes
K6	63	Male	Manufacturing / Education	No	1998	2012	Yes	Switzerland	Yes
K7	61	Male	Media	No	1997	2010	Yes	USA	No
K8	58	Male	IT	No	1994	2012	No	USA	Yes
K9	40	Male	Retail	Yes	1995	2007	No	Germany	Yes
K10	42	Female	Manufacturing	Yes	1994	2010	No	Germany	Yes
K11	59	Female	IT	No	1998	2015	Yes	Austria	No
K12	52	Male	Manufacturing	No	1994	2011	No	Germany	Yes
K13	28	Male	IT	No	1994	2012	Yes	Switzerland	Yes
K14	48	Male	IT	No	1995	2011	Yes	Belgium	Yes
K15	32	Male	Media	No	2000	2012	Yes	Switzerland	No
K16	45	Male	Agriculture	Yes	1998	2015	No	Belgium	Yes
K17	50	Male	Media	Yes	1997	2010	Yes	Norway	No
K18	55	Female	Business support services	No	1996	2009	No	Belgium	Yes

K19	60	Male	Agriculture	No	1998	2008	Yes	Sweden	Yes
K20	55	Male	Manufacturing	No	1994	2008	Yes	United States	Yes
K21	48	Male	Manufacturing	No	1993	2010	Yes	Germany	No
Bosnia and Herzegovina									
B1	34	Male	Agriculture	Yes	1995	2014	No	Belgium	Yes
B2	44	Male	Manufacturing	Yes	1993	2007	No	Belgium	Yes
B3	47	Female	Retail	No	1998	2003	Yes	Germany	Yes
B4	45	Male	Retail	No	1999	2008	No	Germany	Yes
B5	48	Female	Financial services	Yes	1992	1999	No	Germany	Yes
B6	55	Female	Media	Yes	1990	2001	No	United Kingdom	No
B7	60	Male	Manufacturing	No	1990	2004'	Yes	Belgium	Yes
B8	44	Male	Construction	No	1993	2010	Yes	United Kingdom	No
B9	44	Male	Construction	Yes	1991	2012	No	Switzerland	Yes
B10	61	Male	Manufacturing	Yes	1990	2000	No	Norway	Yes
B11	50	Male	IT	No	1991	2000	No	Switzerland	No
B12	52	Female	Agriculture	No	1989	1997	Yes	United Kingdom	No
B13	42	Male	IT	No	1994	2004	Yes	Germany	No
Montenegro									
M1	45	Male	IT	Yes	1990	2007	Yes	Germany	Yes
M2	48	Male	Manufacturing	No	1993	2008	Yes	Germany	No
M3	34	Male	IT	Yes	2000	2010	Yes	Belgium	Yes
M4	38	Female	Financial services	No	2000	2006	No	Switzerland	No

Continued

Table 6.1 Continued

Respondent	Age	Gender	Key Sector of Activity in Kosovo/B&H/ Montenegro	Entrepreneur in Host Country?	Year of Departure	Year of Return	Permanent Residence in Kosovo/B&H/ Montenegro	Host Country	Maintain Investments in Host Country?
M5	35	Male	Construction	No	2002	2007	Yes	Switzerland	No
M6	41	Male	Manufacturing	No	1992	2012	No	Germany	No
M7	57	Female	Tourism	Yes	1991	2015	Yes	United Kingdom	Yes
M8	52	Male	IT	Yes	1990	2015	No	United Kingdom	Yes
M9	48	Male	Tourism	Yes	2000	2008	No	Germany	Yes

minority having all of their business activity in their home country of B&H, Kosovo, or Montenegro. Given that the entrepreneurs had experience living and working abroad, they all had significant international experience. Table 6.2 outlines the key themes derived from the interviews.

The analysis of the interviews captured all instances of the motivations of returnee entrepreneurs, in order to examine why they had chosen to invest in their homeland. From this analysis, monetary and non-monetary motivations were then identified, and illustrate the key elements of individual gains being sought by returnee entrepreneurs. The analysis demonstrated that personal motivations are central to returnee entrepreneurial action. At the same time, a desire to assist the home country to develop is also important, with improving economic and social outcomes for family and friends being a motive. In addition, the underdeveloped economy at home (relative to the host country) can be a determining factor in investing, as there are opportunities for experienced entrepreneurs to exploit. The analysis then sought to understand how these motivations were then translated into action within the home context, demonstrating ties to the location as well as social relationships. The data showed that emotional attachment to the homeland provides an impetus to overcome the institutional challenges that are present. Furthermore, as profit opportunities are superior in the host country, returnee entrepreneurs seek different outcomes associated with activity, and use their international experience for social impact rather than profit. It also shows that family and ethnic ties are used to enable activity at home, with many using informal networks to gain advantages, while some others use formal business networks. Overall the analysis illustrates how the motivations and actions of returnee entrepreneurs lead to gains over time. It shows how returns to self are the key focus of entrepreneurs as they seek to maximise these as activity develops. Their embeddedness in home and host country influences this, and has direct implications for how entrepreneurial strategies are developed. In making strategic decisions, network utilisation enables the liability of foreignness to be overcome.

6.2.2. Embeddedness, Pride, and Returns to Self

The analysis found that when returning to their homeland, a key driver of activity was a sense of pride. When describing their motivations to return, the respondents clearly attributed the decision to invest at home to returns to self, comparing their embeddedness in their home and host countries as a driver for activity. Many described the stability of their lives in their host

Table 6.2 Themes and Illustrative Quotes

Themes	Quotes
'Returns to self' (as primary goal) *Return to homeland motivated by non-monetary considerations*	'At first it was totally emotional. I wanted to go back to invest and help out my family and friends. That completely influenced my investments.' (B7) 'It makes me feel that what I am doing is worthwhile and that I can give something back, I can contribute to things getting better. I am not there to make money. . . . I am pleased that I can contribute to it getting better. I don't need to do it, but it makes me feel proud.' (K5) 'I've made some good money in Germany, but I wanted to come back because this is my home. . . . I had been away too long and my love for the country brought me back.' (M1)
Desire to make a difference and feel pride in oneself	'I didn't need to come back. It was totally emotional. I just wanted to help out in Bosnia and that makes me feel good. I am pleased I can see the difference that my investments are making. I don't need to invest there, I still have businesses in Norway, but it makes me proud that I can help.' (B10) 'There are lots of young people out of work, and with qualifications that are not really helping them find jobs. I came back to help them. If we want them to realise their potential they need to have better opportunities and better training so I am focused on giving them those opportunities: to learn practical skills that they can use to start their own businesses or find good jobs.' (K6) 'I am in a position to help out at home, to create jobs. . . . I just wanted to come back and help, create some new opportunities that weren't there for me when I was young.' (M8)
Homeland investment diversifies portfolio *Profit as secondary motive*	'Making money is always good, but it is not my real aim. I want to expand my activities at home so need to make some. But the opportunities to make money in Bosnia aren't the same as in Belgium so that is not my main focus.' (B2) 'It needs to make money otherwise there are no jobs, but I can use the money I have made abroad to support it even if it makes a loss. . . . I want to make a difference, not make money.' (K9) 'I have made money in the UK, I'm not rich but I have done OK. . . . Coming back to Montenegro is not really about making money for me, it's nice if I do but I want to make other impacts.' (M7)
Profit opportunities superior in host country	'Because the economy is not developed properly the opportunities in Kosovo are not the same as in Switzerland. I want to help to solve some of the problems at home, I am not here to make money because I can stay in Switzerland to do that.' (K6) 'I can make money [in Belgium]. I still have good investments there, and things are easier. It is easier to hire skilled people and build up a business.' (B7) 'Things are settled in Switzerland. I know what I need to do there, what is needed to make a business grow.' (M4)

Table 6.2 *Continued*

Themes	Quotes
Experience working abroad can be applied to home country	'I have done well in Germany, made some money, and still have a number of investments. I've got good experience in the retail sector and can use those skills and the networks I have developed to make good investments in Kosovo.' (K9) 'I have built up my experience [in Germany]. Some of the things I have done there, the businesses I have built up I am trying to do now in Bosnia. It is not as simple but it is working.' (B13) 'I worked for some large companies in Germany, it gave me good skills that I can transfer home. Things like project management, managing people.' (M6)
International experience used to harness social impact	
Feel established and settled in host country	'I had a nice life in Norway. Work was good, things were nice and steady. Sometimes when things are tough I wonder why I came back. . . . But overall it is good. I am from Bosnia, but I am also from Norway. That is where I grew up.' (B10). 'I've had a good life in Germany. It has been positive. I speak the language, got my education there. . . . But I know where I come from, and the circumstances of why I left. I want to help.' (K21) 'I love my life in Germany. It is a big country but I feel at home there. I know the culture and feel that I fit in.' (M2).
Return focused on generating different impacts and outcomes	'There is so much unemployment, and so many challenges for young people [in Kosovo]. My goal is to create opportunities for them.' (K11) 'When I grew up there were lots of tensions, lots of problems. I don't want that for the young people there now. I want them to have a positive future. . . . I want to try to help with that. Things have got better in Bosnia but very slowly. There are still lots of problems. I want to give people opportunities.' (B4) 'There are still lots of problems with things like corruption, and so many challenges for young people. The economy is small and there aren't lots of jobs so people move away. I want to create jobs that help things get better.' (M9)
Family and ethnic ties used to enable activity in homeland	
Desire to assist family and friends who have fewer opportunities	'I want to help my family, they've not found it easy to find jobs. My brother has been in and out of work for a long time. This gives him something to work on and I am proud that I can provide that opportunity. I am pleased that I can help.' (B9) 'My mother has lived here throughout the struggles, throughout the conflict. I want her to see that I am doing something worthwhile and helping out in Kosovo, and that I can help our family. It makes her feel that things are improving, that her son can come home and do something positive.' (K19) 'It is so important to me that I help my family. My brothers and sisters moved back sooner than I did but struggled. . . . I want to be able to help them.' (M7).

Continued

Table 6.2 *Continued*

Themes	Quotes
Contributing to positive ethnic ties provides self-worth	'There are still lots of divisions in Bosnia and they do not seem to be improving. But it makes me determined to help. My people have been persecuted and they still suffer from a lot of inequality, so I want to help them out. It makes me feel good that I can help some of the places that have suffered the most by creating jobs and hope there.' (B5)
	'I want to work with people from different ethnicities, different backgrounds, but it is not easy. Politics gets in the way a lot of the time. It is not easy to work with Serb businesses as there are so many barriers in the way. We are trying but have to rely on our connections with our own people in Kosovo, otherwise it would be too problematic. . . . While we try to develop things with the Serbs, at least we can help our own people.' (K21)
	'We don't have the ethnic tensions that our neighbours have, well not to the same level anyway. . . . Our biggest issue is avoiding corruption and those who are connected to power.' (M6)
Sense of pride and heritage in homeland *Desire to assist homeland development*	'The country has suffered a lot. We are creating a new chapter and I want to help by creating opportunities for people at home. If people see that someone like me can make it work, can make it a success, hopefully it shows them that they can do it too.' (K18)
	'It is not an easy place to do business. It is complicated, there are a lot of unhelpful rules and it is not easy to get approvals for things. But I believe in myself. I have made successful ventures in other countries and want to do it here.' (B6)
	'There are lots of challenges. We didn't suffer so much because of war, but it did impact on the country's ability to grow. Trading with neighbours has not always been easy and things have grown slowly.' (M4)
Feel pride in homeland due to historic links	'When you have moved away from somewhere like Kosovo that is so associated with war and conflict and lots of negative memories, you want to help. I am proud of where I am from and investing in Kosovo makes me feel proud that I am in a position to help other people.' (K1)
	'I still feel very connected to where I am from. Not just the country, but my town and my little village where I grew up. Lots of people where left behind, and lots of people suffered a lot in the war and after it. . . . I am happy to help them by hopefully creating jobs and other opportunities.' (B9)
	'I love my homeland. . . . It is beautiful and I want other people who are not from Montenegro to see the beauty, to see it as a place to visit but also as a place with a good, positive future.' (M8)

Table 6.2 *Continued*

Themes	Quotes
Desire to preserve pride in homeland in younger generation	
Desire to engender pride in homeland in the younger generation so that linkages can be maintained	'I want my children to know where they come from. They may have been born abroad, and feel like Europeans but this is their real home. They don't feel as connected to it as I do as they didn't experience the conflict themselves, but they know our family story, our family history. They know the struggles that we went through and a lot of families like us went through. I want to show that their real home is getting better and that I can contribute to it getting better.' (K20)
	'It is important for my children to know about Bosnia, to understand the past. They are second generation Bosnians that were only born elsewhere because of the war. At first they thought I was crazy going back to invest, telling me that I would just lose money and should stick to what we know in Switzerland. They have had a good life, good education, good jobs. But showing them where they come from, and how I can make it work drives me to succeed in Bosnia.' (B11)
	'My children know where they come from. They have pride in their heritage, not as much as me, but they still see Montenegro as a part of their identity even though they didn't grow up here.' (M8)
Local knowledge provides competitive advantages to returnees	
Knowledge of local context creates opportunities to invest at home	'I have good networks at home with my friends and family, and good business networks in Germany. At home it is more difficult to have the same business networks as there aren't the same businesses in operation. There isn't a group of businesses working on the same things, or a strong supply chain. Our business is quite new to Kosovo. So I have relied on my previous contacts with family and friends. They are not business experts, but they do know what is happening on the ground as many of them stayed during the conflict and after. They can help me make the most of my investments. Having eyes and ears on the ground really helped.' (K12)
	'If I didn't have a good network of family still there I wouldn't have gone back. It would have been too difficult to understand what was going on in terms of how to start a business and then help it grow. Having family still there made me feel that I could make things a success because I could draw on their help.' (B12)
	'Many members of family have gone back or stayed there so I have strong networks. We work together very well, and they have great knowledge of the local environment in terms of what opportunities can be exploited. . . . That has really helped me.' (M6)

Continued

Table 6.2 *Continued*

Themes	Quotes
Underdeveloped economy creates opportunities	'There are still . . . things that need doing, simple services that need to be provided, so there are gaps that can be exploited. It means you have to think about how you can best use your skills and sometimes apply them in businesses that you wouldn't have expected to be involved in.' (K20) Because I had to move quickly when my family emigrated I left behind my previous business and couldn't easily start it again. There was too much competition when I returned for what I wanted to do. . . . So I had to think about how I could help and direct my investments at some of the problems I saw at home, and what the gaps in the market were. . . . I have done things that are completely outside my experience of working abroad, but I have made them work. ' (B10) 'There are lots of opportunities. The economy is so small that lots of things need upgrading and improving. There are lots of challenges but if you are open minded you can find opportunities.' (M7)

country, explaining that this had allowed them to develop skills and networks to benefit their entrepreneurial endeavours. For example: 'I have been there a long time . . . I understand the culture and know how to get things done there' (K20); 'I grew up away from Montenegro really, got all of work experience in Germany and got my education there that helped when I came back' (M1). All stated that they had made money in their host countries through their entrepreneurial and/or employment activity and were now in a position to invest at home.

A key factor in seeking out returns to self was the presence of family and friends in the home country. Indeed, the intimacy of close relationships with family and friends provided the returnee entrepreneurs with a 'warm glow' (Arrow, 1972) and sense of satisfaction. For many of the respondents, having friends and family present in their home country provided them with a desire to invest, so that opportunities could be provided for them.

The attachment to family roots was a key driver shared between the respondents. For some of the respondents, their investments in B&H, Kosovo, and Montenegro allowed them to employ members of their family who were previously unemployed or were in search of better opportunities. Also, the family tie was not necessarily directed at creating job opportunities, but was evident through a desire to help wider society. As one respondent stated: 'Most of my family is still here. My mother is here and in her 80s. She has lived through difficult times and I want her to see that her country is getting better' (K16).

While some stated that they wanted to help their family and friends by creating employment opportunities for them, the majority explained their motivation by describing the pride they gained investing. For example: 'We are a new country that has suffered a lot, and things have been slow to improve. . . . Investing back home provides me with a lot of satisfaction. I have made money in Germany and it has given me lots of opportunities, but nothing compares with the pleasure I get from investing in Kosovo. It is different. It is special' (K10).

The interviewees had a deep sense of pride and altruistic intentions which compelled them to invest at home. The returnee entrepreneurs have strong levels of connectivity and attachment with their homeland (Nielsen and Riddle, 2010). The respondents can compare the institutional environments of their home and host countries, and the entrepreneurial gains associated with each. In describing the differential advantages of home and the host country, the respondents suggested that they did not return because of the entrepreneurial opportunities available at home, often explaining this in terms such as 'things are much better in Europe' (B4) or 'much more stable in Sweden' (K19). This was contrasted with their post-conflict homeland, which was perceived by respondents as unstable with a great deal of uncertainty. While many of the respondents stated that the institutional environments in B&H, Kosovo, and Montenegro had improved since independence, significant issues still remained. In particular, problematic rules and regulations and the presence of corruption were seen as barriers to entrepreneurial development. For example, one respondent stated, 'It is not easy to do business here, it is simpler in the UK . . . but I wanted to challenge myself and do something to benefit my homeland' (M7).

The interviews show that desire for non-monetary gains, pride, and benevolence surpass the desire for profit. These returnees were not particularly seeking business opportunities as they often chose to invest outside of their circle of competencies. Many of the respondents had worked for large multinational enterprises in their host country, and these types of businesses were often not seen to exist at home. As one respondent explained: 'I worked for Siemens for years, but how I can I apply that experience at home? We don't have those types of business here yet' (K12). Despite their embeddedness in the host country leading to employment and/or entrepreneurial opportunities, the respondents selected opportunities at home which do not necessarily correspond to their international experience. Many of the entrepreneurs stated that they had started enterprises or made investments in ventures outside their own area of expertise but in opportunities they felt would have a broad impact on society.

The analysis demonstrates the central importance of being embedded in the activity of returnee entrepreneurs, and how they enable the liability of foreignness to be overcome. However, rather than drawing on formal networks of business or government contacts, the returnee entrepreneurs interviewed draw on informal networks of family and friends. These are often based on *continuity*, reflecting previous networks (Welter et al., 2017b) developed prior to departure, and providing the returnee entrepreneurs with a unique resource from which they can derive emotional gains.

The relational embeddedness associated with networks of family and friends within the home country means that the returnee entrepreneur faces low costs associated with foreignness (Nkongolo-Bakenda and Chrysostome, 2013). The respondents stated that having this network at home meant that it was easier to enter home markets, as well as making it easier to identify and develop opportunities, because they had 'eyes and ears on the ground' (K12) and 'they know everyone and everything' (B2). This can provide the returnee entrepreneur with an advantage over other foreign investors as they can use the network provided by family and friends to develop their own opportunities.

The influence of parents was found to be particularly strong. Parents were seen to have deeply embedded networks in the home country, developed over decades. As one respondent stated: 'My parents know everyone here. People in the government, people in business. . . . If I need a contact I just need to ask them' (K1). Parental ties are important in inducing entrepreneurship (Sorensen, 2007). Not only do they have a sustained impact on the career of the returnee, but they also remit a sense of pride to the returnee. As one respondent stated: 'Most of my family is still here. My mother is here and in her 80s and is proud that I am back and helping. . . . That gives me a great deal of satisfaction' (K7).

These parental ties also work in the opposite direction, with the returnee entrepreneur receiving emotional gains by transmitting their pride to their own children, the second generation of the diaspora. The respondents stated that they gained pride by telling their children of their activities at home, despite the fact that this second generation has less of a connection with the homeland. For example:

My children know their roots, they feel they are partly Kosovar, but also feel German. . . . They have jobs and opportunities in Germany and don't want to come back, but they are proud to see what I am doing. . . . That motivates me to do more and let them see what I am doing in Kosovo. (K5)

It is part of our national pride to pass on stories about the past to our children so they know the history of our country. They see the problems in Bosnia that they don't see where they live in Belgium, but I think they respect me for doing business there. (B7)

The quotes demonstrate that although Nielsen and Riddle (2010) state that relationships with the homeland can be reinforced by previous generations so that a sense of duty is engendered, this does not necessarily extend to encouraging entrepreneurial activity.

The analysis also found evidence of ethnicity-based embeddedness, akin to Qin et al. (2017), who demonstrate that migrants who actively participate in ethnic professional networks are more likely to engage in returnee entrepreneurship. However, the analysis finds that again the emphasis of returnee entrepreneurs is on ethnic ties with family and friends. This was found in all three countries; however, it was more pronounced in B&H. In particular, B&H and Kosovo have ethnic divisions, with Kosovo's northern district of Mitrovica dominated by Serbs and experiencing irregular ethnic clashes, and B&H divided between the predominantly Bosniak Federation and the Serb-dominated Republika Srpska. This means that ethnic ties are pronounced when returning. While these divisions complicate the institutional environment for investment, for the returnee entrepreneurs they can provide an anchor for activity. Like transmission of pride from family and friends, working within ethnic ties also remits emotional gains to the returnee. This is a key aspect of the legacy of war in both countries, with returnee entrepreneurs harnessing their sense of self through working with people from their ethnicity who suffered during the conflicts. As two of the respondents stated: 'It feels great to be doing things in some of the villages that were destroyed . . . it makes me proud that I can help' (B11); 'The people from my hometown suffered a lot and they need help. I am so happy that I am in a position now to help them' (K19). In addition to helping their own ethnic networks, the interviews also found evidence of returnee entrepreneurs trying to overcome ethnic divisions by directing investments outside of their own ethnic ties. For example, one respondent stated that they were planning a new venture in Mitrovica: 'It is difficult to do business there as it is Serb dominated and there are lots of tensions even now, but I want to bring together communities and we are talking to the Serbs' (K20).

6.2.3. The Desire for Emotional Returns and Entrepreneurial Activity

After the establishment of businesses in the homeland, the desire for emotional gains does not cease. Over temporal dimensions, from initial investment to growth, altruistic intentions and a sense of pride remain, yet have an impact on the strategic decisions of the returnee entrepreneurs. While the desire for emotional gains provides an impetus for investment and to overcome the institutional challenges associated with B&H, Kosovo, and Montenegro, these gains are not sufficient to sustain entrepreneurial activity.

The analysis found that the initial motivation of the respondents was an emotional tie which enabled them to make emotional gains. However, over time their international experience is drawn upon as they make strategic decisions about growth. As one respondent explained, 'businesses can't operate on emotions alone, I feel great pride in what I have done, but that isn't enough. We need to be a viable business if we are going to survive' (K1). The returns to self associated with emotional gains combine with a desire to grow ventures so that they can provide a lasting impact.

Over time, activities are often not directed towards profit-making, commercial purposes. Instead, when the desire for emotional gains was still present, making money was not a key motivating factor, and was often a secondary consideration. For example, one respondent stated, 'I haven't made a single euro from my investments in Kosovo, I don't invest here to make money' (K6); while another stated that 'I'm not here to make money, that's not my aim' (M2). Many of the respondents stated that they would have stayed in their host country if they had wanted to prioritise profits, as they would experience less institutional instability and have access to better opportunities. As many of the respondents had business interests in both home and host countries, this provided them with a return on investments abroad which could be reinvested at home.

These views were found to be particularly prevalent among the older respondents (typically over 50 years old) who had more business experience working abroad. Those respondents who had left their home countries before the conflict and had lived abroad for many years had acquired not only experience, but also financial capital that enabled them to reinvest at home without being concerned about making profits there. These respondents stated that the forced nature of their migration had meant they had to abandon previous resources, often leaving behind businesses. This had provided them with the determination to succeed abroad and then reinvest when they had acquired resources to do so. The younger respondents who had often moved away with their parents had left less behind regarding business interests, and acquiring experience and knowledge was a slower process. The majority had attended university abroad and then gained business experience following this, often working in family firms. As they had also acquired less financial capital, they were more insistent that investments at home needed to make money, while at the same time communicating that they were doing so for a sense of pride in helping others, rather than profit being the primary aim.

A key outcome of the desire to maintain emotional gains over time was the direction of activities towards socially beneficial activities. In particular, activities were often focused on trying to solve particular demographic challenges at home. Respondents often stated that given the newborn status of their home country and the long-term effects of conflict, acute demographic challenges were present. Many of the Kosovo respondents stated that the country had a young population and high rates of youth unemployment, as well as a weak education system. This meant that many activities were focused on educational outcomes of the young, again meaning that they often did not correspond to activities they had undertaken in the host country. In B&H, the respondents stated that the key challenge was ethnic divisions, exemplified through the division of the country into the Federation and Republika Srpska. For these respondents, education was also a key element of their ventures, but was often expressed through a desire for historical understanding so that ethnic divisions could be overcome. Often these ventures worked closely with schools and universities to provide training opportunities for students with other young people outside of their own ethnicity. As one respondent stated: 'The danger is that ethnic divisions just become more entrenched over time, so we need to tackle that, and expose people to different ideas and different people . . . we can help bring people together' (B10). As such, while they were embedded at home, there were still significant challenges which networks of family, friends, and co-ethnic ties could not overcome.

6.3. Conclusions

While economic theory has posited the entrepreneur as a monetary profit-maximising individual (Bylund and McCaffrey, 2017), the analysis demonstrates that returnee entrepreneurs to turbulent homelands act to maximise their emotional gains rather than profit. This is a product of embeddedness across borders as superior profit opportunities are available in the host country, but emotional connections to the home country create a desire to invest despite weaker profit opportunities. While it may be the case that entrepreneurial talent is allocated to activities 'with the highest private returns, which need not have the highest social returns' (Murphy et al., 1991, p. 506), these private returns do not necessarily equate to monetary profit. As such, the application of embeddedness describes how change is not driven by purely economically rational individuals, but recognises varied social norms and values (McKeever et al., 2015).

The chapter finds that activities are directed towards social outcomes, which will have an impact on the productivity of entrepreneurial activity as the potential impacts of entrepreneurship such as job creation are reduced. In contrast to Qin et al. (2017), who find that returnee founders can leverage their experience with foreign resources and technological know-how, the chapter shows that international experience plays a reduced role in turbulent environments. Instead of identifying opportunities which build on the returnees' significant international experience, investments are made outside of their technological know-how, and are often directed at social outcomes. Given that the entrepreneurs are not seeking profits which could be reinvested, this will have an impact on the growth of their ventures and the contribution made to economic development.

Although a direct impact on economic growth may not result from such entrepreneurial activity, the returnee entrepreneurs can influence the activity of others at home. This is important as an emerging research stream has analysed the role of returnees in filling entrepreneurial gaps in emerging economies (Li et al., 2012; Qin and Estrin, 2015). Entrepreneurs are not filling gaps of innovation, as Li et al. (2012) find among returnees to fast-growing China. Rather, returnees are sharing capital and expectations of how business should be conducted with family and friends (Williams, 2018). Although the transfer of innovation may be thus reduced, transfers of knowledge will mean that over time, entrepreneurial outcomes in challenging institutional contexts can improve.

This chapter advances understanding of the key influences on investment of returnee entrepreneurs to turbulent institutional environments, furthering understanding of the motivations of highly mobile international entrepreneurs. While entrepreneurship can be defined as the exploitation of opportunities for profit (Bylund and McCaffrey, 2017), this is not necessarily the case when related to returnees to complex institutional environments. Given that these internationally experienced entrepreneurs are able to stay within their more stable host institutional environments, which offer superior profit opportunities, the influence of profit on return to more turbulent environments is reduced.

7

The Impact of Internal Displacement and External Migration on Institutional Trust

7.1. Comparing Internal and External Migration

This chapter examines the trust of institutions among internal and external migrant entrepreneurs. As Chapter 3 demonstrated, trust is an important element in facilitating entrepreneurial action. If entrepreneurs have trust in the prevailing institutions, investment can be secured. Without trust, perceptions of the risks associated with investment will act as a barrier.

The chapter focuses on Bosnia and Herzegovina (B&H), and draws on a population survey and in-depth interviews with entrepreneurs. The chapter finds that external migrant entrepreneurs with international experience have lower trust in institutions than internal migrants. This is explained by the comparison of institutions in the country of origin with more stable institutional environments they experienced while being abroad. The chapter also shows that personal networks have a differential impact on trust, with individuals in more ethnically diverse networks reporting lower trust, reflecting the fact that institutions are not ethnically neutral.

The chapter focuses on two distinct migrant groups: first, the 'traditional' diaspora, which can be defined as having moved across international borders away from their homeland and who maintain a relationship with their country of origin or have returned to their country of origin (Riddle and Brinkerhoff, 2011); second, internally displaced persons, who have not crossed international borders but have moved within their home country to avoid conflict situations and have been cut off from their home city, town, or village. The displaced population often includes some of the most marginalised social groups in society, facing economic and social isolation and poverty (Eastmond, 2006; Turner, 2010). A key distinction between the two groups is that the external migrant diaspora have international experience, gaining from exposure to more developed and stable Western economies, building strong skills,

The Diaspora and Returnee Entrepreneurship. Nick Williams, Oxford University Press (2021). © Oxford University Press.
DOI: 10.1093/oso/9780190911874.003.0007

experience, and networks (Filatotchev et al., 2009), while the internally displaced diaspora have much more limited opportunities. With external and internal migration set to increase in future, due to diverse factors such as climate change, weather shocks, and drought, the dynamics, impacts, and perceptions of these groups requires close attention (World Bank, 2016).

While previous chapters have examined the dynamics of the return of externally displaced migrants, this chapter seeks to compare these with the under-researched group of internally displaced populations. Clearly there are key differences between external and internal migrants, with the internally displaced lacking the international experience and resources of the external diaspora. However, they also cannot be considered as 'traditional' entrepreneurs in the sense that they have the same perceptions and opportunities as the indigenous (non-displaced) population. Indeed, given their experiences of migration, which has been forced due to conflict, they are likely to have different levels of institutional trust as well as reduced opportunities.

Displacement creates a unique context for those affected, as well as significant barriers to opportunity (Cheung and Kwong, 2017). Within internally displaced populations, entrepreneurship may provide a viable option for generating income, enabling individuals to overcome structural employment challenges. Local knowledge and resources will be harder to acquire for internally displaced people due to their relative lack of familiarity with the host location (Cheung and Kwong, 2017). In addition, previous networks can become obsolete due to the rapid departure and dispersion of the population. Bullough et al. (2014) highlight the role of self-efficacy in the creation of entrepreneurial intention in conflict situations; those who are displaced may be less likely to believe that they can succeed as entrepreneurs due to knowledge, resource, and network limitations. As such, the internally displaced may require different strategies towards entrepreneurship in order to overcome these barriers.

The distinction of entrepreneurs based on their migration experience—being external, internal, or non-migrant—can be an important factor in explaining variations of the trust and confidence in institutions of post-conflict environments (Williams and Efendic, 2019). The difference might occur since the external migrant entrepreneurs (i.e. returnees) have gained international experience and skills coming from exposure to more developed and stable institutional environments and Western European markets. By contrast, internally displaced entrepreneurs have much more limited experience and general opportunities to develop their skills and comparative perceptions. Such structural difference between their status and entrepreneurial performance affects their perceptions of the same institutional contexts, leading to a more critical approach of external migrant entrepreneurs. Accordingly, the chapter posits that external migrant entrepreneurs (returnees) have lower trust in their home country institutions in comparison to internal migrant entrepreneurs

7.2. Trust Issues

7.2.1. The Importance of Institutional Trust

Table 7.1 provides a profile of the participants in the in-depth interviews, while Table 7.2 sets out the key questions asked, as well as a summary of responses.

The in-depth interviews found that trust in B&H institutions is very low, with only a small number of respondents reporting positive feedback. The key reason for the low levels of trust was a lack of institutional efficiency, often related to time wasting in regulative processing and burdensome administrative procedures. For example, entrepreneurs report that sometimes '*you must wait for a year to get one document*' (B6); and '*everything is slow . . . you have to wait and wait to get anything done for your business*' (B8). The respondents stated that 'Bosnia has been very slow to reform' and remained an unstable environment in which employees of government institutions are protected, and face no competition or threat for their positions, and thus do not have incentives to improve efficiency.

While such perceptions are not unusual in post-conflict economies (Williams and Vorley, 2017), the interviews also found evidence of differences between the perceptions of internal and external migrants. External entrepreneurs compared the institutional environments to their host countries. For many, the institutional complexity of B&H is something they have not experienced '*after several years of working in different countries*' (B16, B9, B24). For others, this was a challenge because they found that the '*life [in the host country] was too predictable*' (B25) and that the comparative institutional instability in their home country created challenges which were interesting to try to overcome. Rather than putting them off launching an entrepreneurial venture, the institutional environment of B&H provided the impetus to seek a challenge, with emotional ties pulling them back home.

The interviews found that internal migrants were philosophical about the institutional environment, accepting that B&H had generally weak framework

Table 7.1 Profile of Respondents

Respondent	Entity	Sector	Year Company Was Established	Year of Migration	Year of Return	Internal or External Migrant
B1	FBIH	Service	2002	1980	1999	External
B2	FBIH	Service	1999	1992	1999	External
B3	RS	Agriculture	2011	2003	2008	External
B4	FBIH	Industry	1996	1986	1996	External
B5	FBIH	Retail trade	1998	1991	1995	External
B6	RS	Agriculture	2008	1993	1998	External
B7	RS	Retail trade	2002	1992	2000	External
B8	RS	Retail trade	2012	1995	1997	External
B9	RS	Service	2001	1991	2000	External
B10	RS	Retail trade	2012	1992	1997	External
B11	RS	Service	2001	1992	1997	External
B12	FBIH	Service	1996	1992	1995	External
B13	FBIH	Service	1998	1992	1996	External
B14	RS	Food/drink	1994	1993	2005	External
B15	FBIH	Retail trade	1997	1996	2002	External
B16	RS	Service	2003	1995	2003	External
B17	FBIH	Service	2010	2000	2003	External
B18	FBIH	Financial services	2005	Born abroad	2003	External
B19	RS	Food/drink	2005	1995	1995	External
B20	RS	Service	2002	1992	2002	External
B21	FBIH	Service	2011	1992	1996	External
B22	RS	Service	1997	1995	1998	External
B23	RS	Service	1986	1970	1983	External
B24	RS	Food/drink	2008	1979	2009	External
B25	FBIH	Food/drink	2000	2012	2012	External
B26	FBIH	Real estate	2014	2010	—	Internal
B27	FBIH	Counsulting	2010	2006	—	Internal
B28	FBIH	Textile	1988	1973	—	Internal
B29	FBIH	Retail trade	2016	2004	—	Internal
B30	RS	Car repair	2007	1995	—	Internal

Source: Williams and Efendic (2019).

Table 7.2 Summary of Responses of In-Depth Interviews

Key Questions	Summary of Key Responses
What is your level of confidence in institutions?	• If I need to mark my confidence in institutions using the range 1 (minimum) to 5 (maximum), my answer will be 2, maximum 2.5. The main reasons is that I do not see much change in their efficiency. Contrary, our business sector, private sector, has improved a lot over the last few years, which has not been followed by appropriate institutional improvements. The main reason for such trends is a lack of competition in the state institutions. If they know that they can lose a job they would be much more efficient, but in our current institutional setup everyone who is working for these institutions is fully protected and cannot lose his/her job. Without imposing some competition in the institutional sector nothing will change and they will remain inefficient. (B4)
	• After 15 years being in business my experience with government institutions is a little bit better now and I have a bit more confidence than it was the case before. Although there are number of other challenges, I can say, thanks to God, there is some improvement and I am also more confident now. (B18)
	• The trust in institutions depends primarily on the people who provide the services of those institutions. The trust varies because experiences are different. Depending on what day it is, who is that you talk to, and so on, . . . , sometimes you finish what you need quite fast but sometimes it postpones significantly. Currently we have an issue with a client who has started a new business in the field that is new to our region. While trying to obtain licences and register the business we have had a lot of obstacles from the institutions because of the administrative personnel working there did not quite understand the business and they were reluctant to help because of being scared to make a mistake. Also, different employees interpret the Law differently so to complete the same action you often have to go through different procedures. (B27)
	• Generally speaking, the trust is really low. It all depends on what you want to do and who is the responsible person for your action. For example, only [a] few years ago in our municipality you would have to wait days just to get one document. With some improvements, the new governor has shortened these time-wasting procedures significantly. However, still it depends a lot on the administration. (B28)
	• To be honest, people working in our institutions have no clue of how things should be done. I opened two shops and really had a tough time. To put it simply, people working in administration do not know what the next step is after you finish with them and often send you to wrong addresses. So, probably more than half of your visits to institutions will be knocking on wrong doors because of this. This deteriorates the trust significantly. (B29)
	• I have trust in institutions. I did not have any particular problem with them. For example, when I was starting my business I engaged a lawyer who finished all procedures for me in some 15–20 days, and later on I did not have any particular problem. (B30)
What are the main institutional barriers for your business?	• To change and ease the procedures of establishing companies, to code the applications for establishment in order to avoid submitting them under individual name and surname as primary element, because the current way is subject to manipulations. (B4)
	• It is a problem of institutional infrastructure and therefore it is much easier to do business through connections and acquaintances. (B5)

Table 7.2 *Continued*

Key Questions	Summary of Key Responses
	• Well, there were not any particular barriers, people are just talking about it.... (B6)
	• It is a problem that you must wait for a year to get one document. The complete business climate is rather negative. (B8)
	• I would have closed my shop a long time ago had it not been for my relatives from Germany who usually cover my losses. However, this strategy works no more, and unfortunately, I will have to close my shop and emigrate there as well. (B9)
	• The issues were mostly of administrative nature. My husband and I were really surprised about how much time it takes to register a company, especially after several years working at different countries. And the process of finding appropriate employees was also highly time-consuming. (B16)
	• Administration is the worst, definitely the biggest problem. (B17)
	• Well, the bureaucracy should be reduced and the process of opening companies accelerated, and in my opinion, it would be beneficial for attracting the foreign investors if they had certain subsidies during the first years of their investments. (B18)
	• I would like to compare the situation in B&H with the one we have in Switzerland. I receive updated information about activities and events from Switzerland on a regular basis. Here, we cannot offer people anything to inform them about culture and tradition, not even the B&H diaspora. (B24)
	• There are problems in the legal sector, especially when it comes to collecting receivables. Despite having all documentation and judgement on debt collection, it is impossible to implement it. Also, the inspections provide no education at all, they primarily have the purpose of collecting finances. (B24)
Would you recommend to other entrepreneurs from diaspora to invest in B&H? (external migrants only)	• It is only important to have a good business idea because people in B&H are willing to work. (B5)
	• It is logical that the diaspora should invest in B&H. There is a lot of money here (at least in the context of natural resources and potentials). (B8)
	• Unfortunately, two years ago I was in a position that one businessmen asked me for advice to invest 2–3 million of euros in B&H, and I could not say about my positive experience. My opinion is linked to all problems that I faced, and one is that mentality here is not oriented towards entrepreneurship. (B15)
	• It worth investing in B&H but this should be done with trusty people.... I would recommend the diaspora to invest in B&H and the main reason is to keep our resources from foreigners and from destruction. We have so many rivers; if we only work with rivers.... It is sad what we are doing to our forests. (B19)
	• It is the most important that they clued up about the business environment in B&H. And certainly, they will need some support, at least for a few years when they decide to start their business here. You should not expect positive results immediately; it takes time like for everything and everywhere. Probably, joint ventures with domestic partners are the best solution. (B22)
	• I do not recommend investing while the political situation in the country does not change. There is a need to say that it is not only responsibility of politicians, but also of the people living here. (B24)

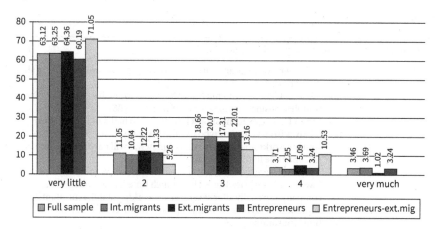

Figure 7.1. Confidence in B&H institutions: an aggregated index for different migrant categories. *Source*: Williams and Efendic (2019).

conditions. Rather than comparing perceptions to other institutional environments, as the external migrants can more readily do, the internal migrants took a more historical view of progress. For example, one stated that '*you can't expect things to change overnight . . . we hoped for the best but things haven't really changed yet, but you never know*' (B29). A lack of progress in terms of institutions was cited by all of the internal migrants as a key factor in holding back entrepreneurship.

The survey also explored differences in perceptions between external and internal migrants. The respondents were asked how much confidence they have in state/entity/municipality institutions, with a scale ranging from 1 ('very little') to 5 ('very much'). The majority of respondents reported that they have very little confidence in these different institutional levels, with 'very little' response chosen by 60%, 59%, and 57% for state, entity, and municipal institutions, respectively. In order to compare these results, Figure 7.1 shows the levels of trust broken down by the full sample, internal migrants, external migrants, entrepreneurs, and non-entrepreneurs. The figure shows that external migrants have lower trust in institutions when compared to non-migrant citizens and internal migrants, while external migrants who are entrepreneurs have the lowest confidence in the sample and in comparison to entrepreneurs in general.

The mean differences[1] of trust in institutions and other relevant variables (age, gender, education, employment, and entrepreneurial status of respondents)

---

[1] We rely on Two-sample t-test with unequal variances to assess the difference between the samples. The tests are implemented in statistical software STATA14 using command *ttesti*.

were then examined for the internal and external migrant subsamples. Compared to internal migrants, external migrants have lower confidence in institutions (–0.08 on a 5-point scale; $p = 0.073$), are more entrepreneurial (there are 2% more entrepreneurs among external migrants; $p = 0.059$), and are also more educated (7% more respondents with secondary and high education; $p = 0.001$). However, the data did not show a significant difference between internal and external migrant samples for employment status, risk aversion, and age variables. These results indicate not only that external migrants are more critical of the institutional environment of their home country once they return, but also that they systematically report or bring higher educational skills and more entrepreneurial activity into the society (identified as relevant experience gained abroad by 23 out of 25 external migrant entrepreneurs). The analysis found that external migrants possess a higher level of human capital and stronger entrepreneurial spirit than internal migrants, and as such provide an 'imported' development potential in this post-conflict society. However, despite this importation, the in-depth interviews found evidence that more efforts need to be made to ensure that the external entrepreneurs' activities can be harnessed. The in-depth interviews found that despite some policy efforts to engage and encourage returnee entrepreneurship, often government was avoided because of trust issues. For example, one respondent stated: *'Politicians can't be trusted. We need a new generation of politicians who are not there because of their connections . . . if government wanted to support my business I would avoid it because I know that they would want a stake in it or a bribe at some point'* (B1).

7.2.2. Individual Characteristics and Trust

To explore the data further, empirical models were used to identify what causes variations in trust for different migrant groups. To estimate these relationships, trust in institutions (*insttrustd*) was used as the dependent variable. To investigate determinants of institutional trust, three types of factors that might be relevant for this post-conflict economy were chosen. Firstly, typical individual characteristics, including potential effects of age (*Age*), gender (*Male*), area of living (*Urban, Suburban*, or *Rural*), educational level (*Educat*), and employment status (*Femploy*) were controlled for. These are all binary variables which are used to make interpretation with marginal effects easier. Although employment status might not be an individual characteristic typically used in similar research, in the context of B&H it can have an important role. Official unemployment is close to 50%, is a key macroeconomic problem in the country, and is also perceived as an institutional failure (Efendic et al., 2011).

The next groups of determinants controlled for are post-conflict specific influences linked to the potential effects of ethnic diversity. There is evidence that the institutional environment had formalised ethnically specific positions during the Bosnian war (Bieber, 2010), and leaving the institutional power under the effective control of the relevant dominant majority in different parts of the country. Accordingly, individuals from the same ethnicity if living in more ethnically homogenous or ethnically diverse areas (*Mixed*) may have different levels of trust in these ethnically governed institutions. At the same time, at the individual level there may be variations in perceptions caused by the more ethnically homogenous or heterogeneous contact networks (*Diversity*) established by these individuals. Previous research has shown that there may be more trust in institutions in ethnically homogenous areas dominated by a majority ethnic group, and consequently, by individuals having ethnically homogenous contact networks (Efendic et al., 2011).

The B&H institutional framework is unique, and includes state level, entity levels (Federation of B&H, Republika Srpska, and the District Brcko of B&H), canton level only in Federation B&H (FB&H) with 10 cantons, and municipal level in both the Federation and Republika Srpska. The District Brcko of B&H is a district in B&H, but is a rather small region in comparison to the entities. The institutional structure in FB&H is much more complex, leading to overlapping jurisdictions and higher direct and indirect costs (Efendic et al., 2011). It is thus important to control for the effect of different institutional structures (*FB&H, RsB&H, DbB&H*) as they may influence the trust in institutions differently. Finally, the analysis controlled for whether respondents were entrepreneurs or not (*Entrepreneur*), and also controlled for the risk aversion of the interviewed individuals (*Risk*), expecting that those who are not willing to take more risk have less confidence in post-conflict established institutions.

Descriptive statistics of variables used in the modelling procedure are presented in Table 7.3. The results of the Probit model, which are estimated with cluster-robust standard errors (to correct the effect of heteroscedasticity identified in the data) are set out in Table 7.4. The table contains marginal coefficients obtained after Probit estimates as they provide useful interpretation. The results are reported for the full B&H sample (Model 1), and sub-samples including migrant population (Model 2) (internal and external migrants together) and then internal migrants who were moving only within B&H (Model 3), and finally, external migrants or returnees (Model 4), i.e. those being abroad and who moved back to B&H. Finally, as part of the robustness procedure the OLS estimate is reported (Table 7.5).

Table 7.3 Descriptive Statistics of Key Variables

Variables	Description of variables	FULL SAMPLE Bosnia and Herzegovina			INTERNAL MIGRANTS only		EXTERNAL MIGRANTS only	
		Number of observ.	Mean	Do not knows/na	No. of observ.	Mean	No. of observ.	Mean
The Dependent Variable								
Insttrust	Institutional trust, factor variable: very little = 1 to very much = 5	5,284	1.70	12.2%	1,355	1.70	491	1.62
Insttrustd	Institutional trust as binary: very little trust = 0; there is some trust = 1	5,284	0.37	12.2%	1,355	0.37	491	0.36
Individual Characteristics								
Age	Age of respondents: 16 to 65 years	6,021	47.10	0.0%	1,555	48.97	536	48.55
Male	Gender: 0 = female; 1 = male	6,021	0.45	0.0%	1,555	0.34	536	0.45
Educat	Education: 0 = no and primary; 1 = secondary and high	5,993	0.71	0.5%	1,551	0.73	534	0.80
Femploy	Employment status: 0 = not employed; 1 = employed	6,004	0.27	0.3%	1,549	0.29	536	0.30
Urban	Urban area: 0 = no; 1 = yes	6,021	0.28	0.0%	1,555	0.32	536	0.36
Suburban	Suburban area: 0 = no; 1 = yes	6,021	0.24	0.0%	1,555	0.31	536	0.29
Rural	Rural area: 0 = no; 1 = yes (base category)	6,021	0.48	0.0%	1,555	0.37	536	0.35

Continued

Table 7.3 Continued

Variables	Description of variables	FULL SAMPLE Bosnia and Herzegovina			INTERNAL MIGRANTS only		EXTERNAL MIGRANTS only	
		Number of observ.	Mean	Do not knows/na	No. of observ.	Mean	No. of observ.	Mean
Institutional Environment								
Fbih	Entity in BiH: 0 = other; 1 = Federation BiH	6,021	0.57	0.0%	1,555	0.50	536	0.54
Rsbih	Entity in BiH: 0 = other; 1 = Republika Srpska (base)	6,021	0.42	0.0%	1,555	0.50	536	0.45
Dbbih	Entity in BiH: 0 = other; 1 = District of Brcko	6,021	0.01	0.0%	1,555	0.01	536	0.01
Ethnic Influences								
Diversity	Personal network is ethnically: 0 = non-mixed; 1 = mixed	4,566	0.55	24.2%	1,145	0.56	408	0.65
Mixed	The area is ethnically: 0 = non-mixed; 1 = mixed	5,831	0.31	3.2%	1,508	0.34	518	0.36
Entrepreneurial Factors								
Entrepreneur	Entrepreneurial status: 0 = non-entrepreneur; 1 = entrepreneur	6,021	0.05	0.0%	1,555	0.05	536	0.07
Risk	Willing to take a risk: 0 = no at all; 1 = ready to take some risk	5,563	0.70	7.61%	1,424	0.71	505	0.74

Table 7.4 Determinants of Institutional Trust: Probit Cluster-Robust Estimate, Marginal Effects Reported

Variable	Model 1 Full Sample for B&H	Model 2 Migrant Subsample	Model 3 Internal Migrants	Model 4 External Migrants
Individual Characteristics				
Age	−0.003***	−0.003**	−0.004***	−0.001
Male	−0.024	−0.004	−0.010	0.022
Educat	0.005	−0.033	−0.036	−0.015
Femploy	0.052***	0.118***	0.118***	0.114*
Urban	−0.018	0.034	0.039	0.034
Suburban	−0.032	−0.046	−0.071*	0.024
Institutional Environment				
Fbih	−0.108***	−0.100***	−0.082**	−0.130***
Dbbih	0.030	−0.073***	−0.055*	−0.037
Post-Conflict Ethnic Influences				
Diversity	−0.002	−0.050	−0.001	−0.195***
Mixed	−0.027	−0.040	−0.013	−0.010*
Entrepreneurial Factors				
Risk	0.155***	0.146***	0.141***	0.182***
Entrepreneur	−0.027	−0.047	0.002	−0.181**
Model Diagnostics				
No. of observations	3,834	1,297	937	360
Wald test (p-value)	0.000	0.000	0.000	0.000
Hosmer-Lemeshow test (p-value)	0.10	0.25	0.58	0.65
Predicted probability	0.38	0.38	0.38	0.37

The dependent variable is *Insttrustd*: very little trust = 0; there is some trust = 1.

***, **, * denote statistical significance of the estimated coefficient at the 1%, 5%, and 10%, respectively.

Note: the variable of particular interest '*entrepreneur*' obtained the p-value of 0.018.

Source: Williams and Efendic (2019).

Table 7.5 Determinants of Institutional Trust: OLS Cluster-Robust Estimate

Variable	Model 1 Full Sample for B&H	Model 2 Migrant Subsample	Model 3 Internal Migrants	Model 4 External Migrants
Individual Characteristics				
Age	−0.002***	−0.002**	−0.003**	−0.001
Male	−0.023	−0.002	−0.008	0.023
Educat	0.004	−0.034	−0.037	−0.019
Femploy	0.050***	0.113***	0.113***	0.100*
Urban	−0.016	0.035	0.040	0.048
Suburban	−0.029	−0.043	−0.065*	0.021
Institutional Environment				
Fbih	−0.104***	−0.096***	−0.077**	−0.157***
Dbbih	0.028	−0.074***	−0.054*	−0.079
Post-Conflict Ethnic Influences				
Diversity	−0.001	−0.002	−0.003	−0.184***
Mixed	−0.024	−0.039	−0.012	−0.101*
Entrepreneurial Factors				
Risk	0.151***	0.141*	0.133***	0.178***
Entrepreneur	−0.026	−0.046	−0.005	−0.178**
Model Diagnostics				
No. of observations	3,834	1,297	937	360
F-test (p-value)	0.000	0.000	0.000	0.000
R-squared	0.04	0.05	0.05	0.10
Ramsey RESET test (p-value)	0.99	0.51	0.96	0.67
Variance Inflation Factor test (mean)	1.11	1.15	1.15	1.18

The dependent variable is *Insttrustd*: very little trust = 0; there is some trust = 1.

***, **, * denote statistical significance of the estimated coefficient at the 1%, 5%, and 10%, respectively.

Note: the variable of particular interest '*entrepreneur*' obtained the p-value of 0.029. The constant is estimated but not reported in the table.

Source: Williams and Efendic (2019).

Beginning with individual characteristics, the data show a very stable and positive influence of employment status in all estimated models (Models 1–4). Those who are employed report systematically more trust in institutions in comparison to those who are not employed or who are outside of the labour force. Such a result implies that a better economic status of individuals influences their trust in institutions. Related to this, the in-depth interviews found evidence of a perception that unemployment was a cultural, as well as an economic, problem. Trust in institutions among the employed was linked to the perception that institutions were blamed for unemployment by others. However, a 'Balkan mentality' meant that people were not prepared to do low-paid jobs, rather than it being an institutional issue. One respondent stated that *'[young people] would do menial jobs abroad but won't do it at home because they want their friends and family to think they are a success, with a good wage, nice car, things like that'* (B1). Despite this, the analysis found that the effect of age is significant and negative in all models (Models 1–3) but not for the ex-diaspora members (Model 4). A negative coefficient implies that older respondents report lower trust in institutions in comparison to the younger respondents.

In terms of the effect of institutional environment, the data show a negative, high, and significant effect of FB&H entity in all models. Respondents from FB&H report around 10% systematically lower trust in comparison to respondents from the Republika Srpska. This outcome is not surprising given that institutional structure in FB&H is more complex. The finding also shows issues in coordination and functioning of FB&H, which can be reflected in the trust of these institutions. A more complex institutional setup decreases confidence in institutions, which also means that there is greater need for structural institutional reforms in this entity.

The coefficients estimated for post-conflict ethnic influences were found to be significant in the external migrant sample only. This suggests that respondents living in more diverse areas and having more diverse ethnic networks are systematically (20%) less confident in institutions than those having more homogenous networks. Ethno-established institutions which are governed by majorities are likely to receive more trust in ethnically homogenous areas and by individuals having such personal homogenous networks, rather than in ethnically diverse environments and from individuals establishing such personal contacts. Although the marginal effect of ethnic diversity in the area of living is significant, it is small (1%), which suggests that individual network diversity is the main effect on institutional trust.

Finally, the data show a consistent and high effect of personal risk aversion in all estimated models. Respondents being ready to take more risk, which can be considered to be a general feature of entrepreneurs, report 15% better trust in institutions, on average. This links to evidence from the in-depth interviews that there were always risks to entrepreneurial activity but that they could be overcome; for example: *'nowhere is it 100% guaranteed that your business will succeed . . . there are problems everywhere that you have to overcome'* (B25), and *'there are challenges and there are risks, but I want to make it work so I am determined to overcome them'* (B22). In addition to this, while the effect of entrepreneurial status is not significant in other models, once it is estimated for ex-diaspora entrepreneurs (Model 4), this variable has a significant negative effect, and a rather high magnitude of 18%. Simply, ex-diaspora entrepreneurs report systematically lower trust in institutions in comparison to non-entrepreneurs.

Further results can be obtained by looking at the combined effects of different determinants in the model. Interactions between entrepreneurial status and ethnic diversity influence were examined, as this has been specifically linked to external migrants (Model 4). Although entrepreneurial status does have a high individual effect (0.18), when combined with personal network diversity (*Diversityd*) it decreases trust in institutions quite significantly (combined marginal coefficient is –0.32, p-value = 0.001). For example, entrepreneurs having ethnically diverse network have 32% less trust in institutions than non-entrepreneurs having ethnically homogeneous networks.

7.3. Conclusions

This chapter has examined the perceptions of institutions of internal and external migrants. The chapter focuses on B&H, which experienced significant internal and external migration. The in-depth interviews found that external migrants have a strong emotional tie to B&H, which gives them a desire to assist in the future development of the country. This means that despite the inherent institutional challenges they face, and which compare negatively with the stable institutional environments that the external migrants experienced in more developed economies, migrants are not deterred from launching entrepreneurial ventures.

The chapter finds that international external migrants have lower trust in institutions in comparison to internal migrants. This can be explained by their exposure to other institutional environments. Many of the external migrants have been based in Western economies with much more stable institutions, which provide a cognitive contrast with the institutions in B&H. While these external migrants will have gained valuable skills and experience (Riddle and Brinkerhoff, 2011), they also have gained insight into the deficient institutions at home. Improving B&H institutions following standards of developed European economies is a priority that will increase trust and entrepreneurship activities by diaspora members.

The findings also demonstrate how personal networks have a differential impact on perceptions. Individuals with more ethnically diverse networks report lower trust in institutions. While the reasons for this finding are complex, the chapter posits that it is a result of the fragmented political and institutional system in B&H, as institutions are often not ethnically neutral throughout the country. For example, the political division between the Federation of B&H and Republika Srpska maintains a stark reminder of previous tensions as well as perpetuating the partition of institutions. Networks are of crucial importance to migrant entrepreneurs who are either returning to their homeland or who have been internally displaced. While networks vary in size, location, and benefit (Smallbone et al., 2010), they provide access to resources that are unavailable to outsiders. While more diverse networks are generally regarded as beneficial for business development, if there is an institutional discrimination based on ethnicity, the effect of diversity might diminish.

8

Engaging Returnee Entrepreneurs Through Institutional Change

8.1. The Challenge of Engagement

The previous chapters have all demonstrated the important role that institutions play in harnessing returnee entrepreneurship, influencing the perceptions and trust of entrepreneurs as well as the activities they undertake. In this chapter, the analysis returns to the role of policy making in developing institutions which can secure returnee investment. The chapter demonstrates that despite the importance attached to the diaspora in policy discourse, they are an under-utilised resource in economic and social development. Policy is fragmented, meaning that progress in terms of engagement with the diaspora has been limited.

The chapter is based on interviews with policy makers and key stakeholders involved in the development of diaspora and economic development policies, as well as provision of business support, in B&H, Kosovo, and Montenegro (see Table 8.1 for profiles of the respondents). The chapter demonstrates how institutional changes are being driven by acute development challenges within the country. Part of the perceived solution to these challenges is the effective mobilisation of diaspora entrepreneurs who can bring investment and vital skills back home. The chapter shows that diaspora-specific institutional change has been slow to develop in the three countries. Improving linkages through voting rights and status are at early stages of development, despite their potential importance (Waldinger, 2015; Weinar, 2017). However, the institutional framework is being reformed to try to mobilise the potentially highly valuable resource of diaspora entrepreneurs more effectively. The policy emphasis has been on improving the general institutional environment, so that perceptions of the entrepreneurial opportunity can improve; but this also requires policy makers to develop more coordinated and targeted support. Yet this is challenging, given that many first-generation diaspora entrepreneurs returned following independence and then left again

The Diaspora and Returnee Entrepreneurship. Nick Williams, Oxford University Press (2021). © Oxford University Press.
DOI: 10.1093/oso/9780190911874.003.0008

Table 8.1 Profile of Respondents

Respondent	Organisation	Role
Kosovo		
K1	Office of the Prime Minister	Development of economic development policy, including diaspora-related institutional change
K2	Ministry of Diaspora	Development of diaspora engagement policies and strategies; working closely with other government departments
K3	American Chamber of Commerce	Supporting indigenous and diaspora entrepreneurs
K4	Business Support Organisation	Supporting diaspora entrepreneurs to return fully or invest in their home country
K5	Economic Development Consultant	Advising government on institutional change
K6	Chamber of Commerce	Supporting indigenous and diaspora entrepreneurs
K7	Office of the Prime Minister	Development of economic development policy, including diaspora-related institutional change
K8	Chamber of Commerce	Supporting indigenous and diaspora entrepreneurs
K9	Chamber of Commerce	Supporting indigenous and diaspora entrepreneurs
K10	Business Support Organisation	Supporting diaspora entrepreneurs to return fully or invest in their home country
K11	American Chamber of Commerce	Supporting indigenous and diaspora entrepreneurs
K12	Business Support Organisation	Supporting diaspora entrepreneurs to return fully or invest in their home country; advising government on institutional change
Bosnia and Herzegovina		
B1	Business support organisation	Supporting diaspora entrepreneurs to return fully or invest in their home country
B2	United Nations Development Programme	Developing programmes and investment to foster diaspora return and investment; working with government departments on developing policy
B3	Ministry for Human Rights and Refugees of Bosnia and Herzegovina	Development of economic development policy, including diaspora-related institutional change
B4	Ministry for Human Rights and Refugees of Bosnia and Herzegovina	Development of economic development policy, including diaspora-related institutional change
B5	Ministry for Human Rights and Refugees of Bosnia and Herzegovina	Development of economic development policy, including diaspora-related institutional change

Continued

Table 8.1 *Continued*

Respondent	Organisation	Role
B6	Business support organisation	Supporting diaspora entrepreneurs to return fully or invest in their home country; advocacy of diaspora to government
B7	Chamber of Commerce	Supporting indigenous and diaspora entrepreneurs
Montenegro		
M1	Directorate for Diaspora	Development of economic development policy, including diaspora-related institutional change
M2	Chamber of Commerce	Supporting indigenous and diaspora entrepreneurs
M3	Business support organisation	Supporting diaspora entrepreneurs to return fully or invest in their home country; advocacy of diaspora to government
M4	Directorate for Diaspora	Development of economic development policy, including diaspora-related institutional change
M5	Ministry of Foreign Affairs	Development of economic development policy, including diaspora-related institutional change

due to institutional challenges, and now often only engage through low-value remittances; while the second generation are harder to engage and assimilate as they have less of an emotional tie to the home country (Williams, 2020).

8.2. Policy Priorities and Institutional Change

8.2.1. Challenges at Home

Table 8.2 sets out the interview schedule used and the summary of responses for each country. The findings show that the countries are caught between the isolation and assimilation of diaspora entrepreneurs, in part caused by an un-developed institutional environment as well as uncoordinated reforms. While diaspora entrepreneurs provide remittances, they are often economically isolated from their home country, with perceptions of risk acting as a bar-rier to investment. The respondents were unanimously clear about the acute economic, social, and demographic challenges facing each of the countries, which mean that the requirement to engage the diaspora is pressing. In partic-ular, respondents stated that demography was forcing institutional reforms. For example, in Kosovo the young and emerging population was cited as a

Table 8.2 Interview Questions and Summary of Responses

Question	Summary of Responses		
	Kosovo	Bosnia and Herzegovina	Montenegro
1. What are the current economic challenges facing your country?	Demographic issues associated with young population but low levels of job creation; low levels of entrepreneurial activity; continued migration of skilled and entrepreneurial people.	Low economic growth; low levels of entrepreneurial activity; continued migration away from B&H; Ethnic divisions within B&H.	Small population and low growth; low levels of entrepreneurial activity; localised business activity.
2. How can engagement of diaspora entrepreneurs assist in solving these challenges?	More entrepreneurship and investment from diasporas would create employment, increase productivity, and influence others into action; demonstration effect important as levels of entrepreneurship are low; diaspora entrepreneurs have higher skill levels than entrepreneurs based in Kosovo.	More entrepreneurship required for job creation, especially for young population; diaspora can fill skills gaps and influence activity of other people.	More entrepreneurship is required for job creation; need diaspora to bring skills home and act as role model to others; returnees can improve ambition of entrepreneurs at home.
3. How have institutions changed to mobilise and attract diaspora entrepreneurs?	Institutions have changed rapidly since independence; transitioned from central planning and aimed to create open market economy; Kosovo characterised by unstable institutions, with corruption a particular challenge; government has been slow to engage with diaspora, but changing with Ministry of Diaspora and new policy initiatives; coordinated policies now emerging through National Development Strategy and associated actions.	Institutions have changed but positive change has been slow; B&H still characterised by unstable institutions; difference in institutions between Federation and Republika Srpska is problematic; government has started to emphasise potential of diaspora in policy yet many still see risks to investment at home.	Institutions have improved but positive change has been slow; more emphasis on the diaspora in policy.

Continued

Table 8.2 *Continued*

Question	Summary of Responses		
	Kosovo	Bosnia and Herzegovina	Montenegro
4. What are the key barriers facing diaspora entrepreneurs wishing to return and/or invest in your country?	Perceptions of risk is biggest challenge; as formal institutions have been slow to become embedded, informal institutions have been slow to catch up.	Perceptions of risk; institutions at home viewed as unstable and unsupportive of investment.	Perceptions of risk, especially associated with corruption.
5. What are the key institutional changes being made to engage diaspora entrepreneurs in economic activity at home?	Focus has been on attracting remittances, although this has limited potential due to low levels; privatisations attracted many diaspora entrepreneurs home, however many left again due to institutional challenges; questions about the success of privatised enterprises.	Specific programmes such as TOKTEN have been used, yet have limited long-term impact.	Policy attempts to create more stable institutions; creation of specific government departments, however they are very small and attract very limited funding.
6. What are the common perceptions of opportunity among diaspora entrepreneurs?	View institutional environment as inherently risky; perceptions of corruption still act as a barrier despite improvements being made.	Institutional environment is viewed as being risky; Yet opportunities at home have expanded as economy has grown.	Risks associated with corruption; Small market size means that opportunities are seen as limited.
7. What actions are being taken to improve perceptions of diaspora entrepreneurs?	Public media campaigns, for example anti-corruption; courts being pushed to be more proactive in tackling corruption; PR campaign from government to communicate institutional improvements; attempts to set up digital registry of diaspora.	Ministry is seeking to communicate and actively engage with the diaspora, but progress is slow; steps taken to tackle corruption.	Policy efforts to tackle corruption, yet progress is slow and not led to improved perceptions yet; more communication with the diaspora.

Table 8.2 *Continued*

Question	Summary of Responses		
	Kosovo	Bosnia and Herzegovina	Montenegro
8. What are the key mechanisms for institutional change?	Ministry of Diaspora; Office of the Prime Minister; National Development Strategy; numerous support agencies, including Chambers of Commerce and private sector consultants advising government and diaspora entrepreneurs.	Responsibility lies within Ministry for Human Rights and Refugees of Bosnia and Herzegovina; no dedicated policy for engaging with diaspora.	Directorate for Diaspora within the Ministry of Foreign Affairs, and a Strategy of Cooperation with Diaspora and a Strategy for Integrated Migration Management in Montenegro.
9. What actions are being taken to learn from institutional change and diaspora engagement in other countries?	NDS is informed by consultations with international partners, including IMF and EU; need to do more to learn from neighbours, although isolated political situation acts as a barrier to genuine knowledge sharing.	Some policy learning from neighbours, for example through TOKTEN; some engagement with external partners on developing approaches, however B&H is viewed as unique in terms of its political landscape, so different policy approaches are required.	Some policy learning from other countries, but limited application due to lack of investment.
10. What are the current institutional priorities for engaging diaspora entrepreneurs?	Need for more coordinated policy; more awareness of who the diaspora are and where they are based; more engagement of diaspora in institutional building so that policies are informed.	Need more investment and priority given to diaspora specific policy; more involvement of diaspora in policy making; requirement for Federation and Republika Srpska to work together more positively.	More investment needed so that coordinated and sustained policies can be funded.
11. What actions are being taken to involve diaspora in political decision-making?	Key challenge due to political fragmentation of Kosovo; challenge is for parliament to agree for reserve seats to be devoted to diaspora.	Political fragmentations means that involving diaspora is difficult; little direct involvement.	Limited action taken; some attempts to engage but lack of investment.

challenge: 'we have 30,000 18 year olds every year, but only 20,000 new jobs being created ... the economy is not sustainable' (K10); and 'we are a post-war, post-socialist country with a young population and not enough jobs ... we need to bring in all the expertise we can' (K4). Similarly, in both B&H and Montenegro, policy makers and other stakeholders stated that having young, and relatively small, populations meant that reforms were necessary to support development. This has led to increasing consideration of reforms which support entrepreneurial activity at home, especially activity which enables greater trade across borders; for example: 'We are a small country on the edge of Europe ... we need to link more to the outside because domestic markets are so small' (M3). Furthermore, in B&H conflict has left a legacy of a divided country with ethnic tensions remaining a key concern: 'We are divided. We need reforms which bring together the Bosniak and Serb populations and attract people home, but the history of divisions means progress has been very slow, if not non-existent' (B4). Policy makers in B&H stated that there had been attempts to bring together the Bosniak-dominated Federation and Serb-dominated Republika Srpska to work together on formulating diaspora policy, but that politicians in Republika Srpska had always refused to take part. In fact, Republika Srpska had developed their own diaspora policies, which, as some of the interviewees stated, refer to Serbs only and refer to Serbia as the homeland, including for Bosnian Serbs. Such policy developments do little to bring together policy under one unified national umbrella.

In addition to internal challenges, some of the policy emphasis within the three countries is influenced by EU accession ambitions. As Chapter 4 outlined, Montenegro is an official candidate country for EU accession, while B&H and Kosovo are not official candidates but have EU accession as specific elements within foreign policy. Stakeholders recognised that a desire to move closer to the European Union influenced a great deal of domestic policy. Yet, in terms of diaspora and returnee policies, they also highlighted critical tensions in policy making. Many stakeholders explained that migration policies often put them in conflict with EU policy makers. Conversations with the European Union have impressed on policy makers in B&H, Kosovo, and Montenegro that migration policy is considered to be an internal issue, and that issues within the Balkans are not a priority for European-wide policy making. For example, one policy maker stated, 'The EU migration policies focus on host countries and are set up to benefit the large dominant countries. They see migration, the diaspora, trying to get people to return as an internal issue, something for domestic policy' (K7); while another said that 'EU countries, especially Germany, have recruited a lot of low skilled, low paid labour from Bosnia. They are happy to do that. But if [we] then try to attract them back, it doesn't make them very happy' (B3). As a result of these policy tensions, the interviews found evidence of engagement with the European Union and accession requirements, yet also recognition that policy needed to be created internally which not only contributes to development but also slows down brain drain away from the Balkans. The stakeholders all stated that national-level policy was needed to engage with the diaspora in order to help tackle demographic challenges.

8.2.2. Formal Institutional Change and Returnee Entrepreneurship

For countries aiming to engage with their diaspora, a key area of institutional focus is on how to attract remittances, as the total size of remittances can be a significant element of GDP. While remittances can alter the local balance of economic and political power (Brinkerhoff, 2011), in the small economies of B&H, Kosovo, and Montenegro, the value and potential impact are small, despite the total amount being large. The respondents explained that as a total figure, the level of remittances meant that government would naturally focus on it, but when filtered down to remittances to individuals or families, due to their small size they were used for consumption rather than investment. Typical responses were:

> The reality is that remittances are very small. People are probably sending back something equivalent to a minimum wage, maybe €200 a month. It is only enough for people to try to survive on, just using it to feed themselves. They aren't going to put it to use developing a new business. That is what governments often want but it is removed from reality. (K10)

> Most of the remittances go to families, go to households. The amounts are fairly small for a family and aren't invested in businesses or other opportunities. . . . Most of it is just helping them to survive. (B5)

The quotes demonstrate that while the productive potential of remittances is a common focus for policy makers, often the ability of remittances to influence economic development is limited. Respondents often stated that the focus on remittances is changing, albeit slowly; for example: 'government has focused too long on remittances and say that they were not being used productively. It keeps getting repeated [in government policy] but has little real potential impact' (K8); 'remittances are still seen as important and a key part of our strategy, but we are also starting to think of new ways of engaging the diaspora' (M1).

While remittances were utilised as part of economic development strategy during the conflicts of the 1990s, especially in Kosovo, their contribution to peace-building, reconstruction, and post-conflict development has been questioned (Brinkerhoff, 2011; Williams, 2018). The stakeholders stated that there was a need to move away from the view that remittances were an answer to economic development challenges, and what was required was a clearer focus on effective institutional reform. The emphasis on remittances was seen by the respondents as being symptomatic of a tendency to downgrade genuine institutional reform which would engage the diaspora entrepreneurs and lead to higher levels of investment and entrepreneurial activity at home.

In addition to the focus on remittances, a key element of institutional reform has been privatisation, which has remained a priority of transition and post-conflict economies seeking higher levels of entrepreneurship (Williams and Vorley, 2015, 2017). The respondents stated that much of diaspora entrepreneurial activity seen in the immediate post-independence period was related to the privatisation of former state-owned enterprises, and while some diaspora entrepreneurs stayed and continued to run these enterprises, many returned to their host country or withdrew investments. The respondents explained that this meant that much of the activity associated with privatisation did not focus on creating new ventures, and that at the same time there was very little obligation placed on the entrepreneurs regarding what should be done after privatisation. As one respondent stated: 'There was no requirement on the entrepreneurs regarding what do with privatised businesses, so there was a lot of asset stripping which undermined the longer term viability of those businesses' (K12). Another respondent argued that the entrepreneurs taking over the privatised businesses often had little experience: 'Often the entrepreneurs have not known what to do with previously government owned businesses. Entrepreneurs took previously successful businesses, that were successful before the war, and sold parts off . . . they took machinery and sold it and didn't know what to do next with the business' (M3).

Diaspora entrepreneurs are often viewed by policy makers as possessing valuable skills that can be transferred home to promote higher levels of entrepreneurship in their home country (Riddle et al., 2010). The respondents stated that the privatisations during early independence failed to harness diaspora entrepreneurship for two key reasons: first, the levels of skills and experience of those returning; and second, the unstable institutional environment. With regards to skills and experience, the interviews found that different generations of diaspora entrepreneurs were seen to have different potential impacts on the economy. The first generation, who moved prior or during the war, were viewed by many of the respondents as having relatively low levels of skills and therefore possessing a lower potential impact on the economy. One respondent explained that post-independence the first generation were attracted back to the country due to their strong emotional ties, but this did not mean that Kosovo was gaining through their entrepreneurial skills:

> The first generation came back, but look at what they did abroad. Most of them owned restaurants, bars, cafes, clubs. We already had plenty of those, so what knowledge can they apply back home? (K10)

The issue of the skills of the diaspora and how it could contribute to the home economy was also raised by other stakeholders. Another respondent explained that 'very few diaspora were entrepreneurs before 1999, but they realised they had to work for themselves when they moved to create their own opportunities' (B6); while another said, 'People took whatever jobs they could find, some became entrepreneurs but certainly not the majority. . . . They were generally in low skilled jobs which impacted what they could do when they came home' (M4). In contrast, the second generation, who were born abroad and are more embedded within their host country, were viewed as having higher levels of skills, gained through their international business experience, and therefore present a greater potential impact on the economy. Yet, at the same time, these second-generation diaspora entrepreneurs have much weaker emotional ties to their homeland. As two respondents explained: 'They come in the summer and spend money in the nightclubs, they come at Christmas to visit family, but that is about it. They don't want to invest' (K11); 'they come to holiday, are proud of their roots but not so much that they want to move back or invest' (M5).

The second generation has a weaker emotional tie in part due to growing up abroad, but also because they are living and working in countries with stable economies, and thus where there are much lower risks for entrepreneurs. One respondent stated that 'they are coming from societies were rules are much more stable, where the rule of law is much more established' (K1), while another said that because of this, 'why would they want the risk of starting a business here?' (B7). As such, harnessing the different generations of diaspora entrepreneurs requires different institutional approaches.

The focus on remittances and privatisation has meant that since independence, institutional change related to diaspora entrepreneurs has been underdeveloped and uncoordinated. However, as Chapter 4 demonstrated, policies and strategies are being developed to further mobilise the diaspora, moving from the focus on remittances to higher levels of engagement in investment.

In B&H there is no existing dedicated policy for diaspora engagement, although the 'Strategy on Migration and Asylum of Bosnia and Herzegovina' and the 'Action Plan 2016–2020' focuses on strengthening the institutional and policy frameworks for the purpose of linking diaspora and economic development (Ministry of Security, 2016). However, as many of the stakeholders noted, such frameworks 'are very broad, talking about general strategies, but they don't really tackle the key challenges' (B5). In Kosovo, the National Development Strategy (NDS) contains policies and strategies to mobilise the activities of the diaspora to benefit the economy (Government of Kosovo, 2016). While in Montenegro, whose policy is the most coordinated of the three countries, there is a Directorate for Diaspora within the Ministry of Foreign Affairs, and a Strategy of Cooperation with Diaspora and a Strategy for Integrated Migration Management in Montenegro (Government of Montenegro, 2014). The respondents explained these policy developments as attempts to tackle domestic challenges that also reflect a desire to engage with the diaspora more effectively: 'policymakers are trying . . . we need more investment, and our diaspora can help' (M2).

Kosovo's NDS calls for a Homeland Engagement Programme to be established which will allow the short-term deployment of diaspora experts and students in public, educational, and private companies through subsidies; and that a TOKTEN scheme needs to be established. These institutional changes were generally welcomed by the stakeholders, who felt that they represented progress in policy; however, there was concern that much of the reforms were short term: 'we are trying to bring back entrepreneurs and academics to share knowledge but they are only supported for short periods, there are no long-term incentives' (K4). Yet the interviews found evidence that longer term institutional changes were being made; for example, one respondent stated that a matching grants scheme was being developed in collaboration with the United Nations Development Programme. Such programmes have been difficult to develop in Kosovo, in part due to 'budget constraints which mean we have limited capacity to offer incentives' (K9), but also because of pressure from international agencies. One respondent explained that 'if the government started offering financial incentives for the diaspora to invest, the international partners working here would object. . . . The IMF would not approve of incentives where little has been done to tackle economic challenges' (K8). Given the significant role of international agencies in economic and social policy making in Kosovo, as well as structural loans from the IMF, such pressure has a significant impact on institutional change. Tax breaks have been introduced for diaspora investments, giving breaks of between three to seven years, depending on how many jobs are being created. This formal institutional reform received objections: 'our international partners objected, they said "why haven't you tackled the informal economy before you start offering tax breaks", but we managed to get it through' (K3), while another said: 'there is pressure from EU not to do it because they want us to tackle other challenges like corruption . . . they were not happy but gave permission' (K5).

B&H took part in the TOKTEN scheme, which received a great deal of government exposure as part of efforts to encourage highly qualified members of the diaspora living abroad to link with the homeland. However, policy makers involved in assessment of its impacts stated that it had some short benefits but did not lead to longer linkages between external and internal actors. Similar schemes have also been attempted; however, many of the interviewees stated that this had resulted in a piecemeal approach to policy. As one stated: 'We've been waiting for the grand strategy from government so that the diaspora feel welcomed back, "here are the tax breaks, here are the cuts to administration, we love you, please come back", but we haven't had it' (B6). Instead, policy had suffered from a 'three steps forward, two steps back' (B1) approach, with little real progress made.

Despite policy being most co-ordinated in Montenegro under the Directorate for Diaspora, this has not led to real policy change being implemented. Many policy initiatives, such as a Fund for Diaspora, which aims to link migrant communities with businesses at home, have yet to be rolled out. As one respondent said: 'The will is there [to engage the diaspora], they want to do something, but there isn't the funding behind it. . . . It is a small part of government and not really a priority' (M3).

8.2.3. Changing Perceptions of Institutions

A key challenge for all three countries has been changing the perceptions of diaspora entrepreneurs so that they can be attracted home. Constantly changing rules associated with the evolving institutional environments has made planning difficult, but has also meant that perceptions are generally negative about the risks associated with investment. In particular, there have been concerns about corruption in B&H, Kosovo, and Montenegro. Typical quotes were: '[corruption] is the number one worry of the diaspora' (K7); 'corruption is real, it has not gone away, and the diaspora are concerned about it' (B2); and 'when you are asking people to invest in their homeland they want to know it is safe . . . for most people it is, but many people have a nagging worry about corruption' (M3). The interviewees explained that while institutional reforms had been enacted to try to tackle and reduce corruption, it remained a fact of life in the Balkans.

Tales of corruption faced by the diaspora were provided by many respondents as illustrative examples of why perceptions of institutional change have not improved. One respondent said that 'entrepreneurs would come back, try to set up a business but then someone would come along and say "what's in it for me?" So they had to bribe if they wanted to survive' (K10). Others stated that 'there has been blackmail and lots of uncertainty . . . with many diaspora entrepreneurs ending up feeling it wasn't worth the effort' (B7), or that 'there has been violence, intimidation, people being bullied back out of the country' (K11). The respondents stated that diaspora communities were very close-knit, and if one member had a bad experience the rest would soon learn about it.

Privatisation programmes have also proved fertile grounds for corruption. The privatisation of Kosovo's state-owned enterprises was a key element of the United Nations Mission in Kosovo (UNMIK) strategy to develop a more open market economy. Knudsen (2010) has noted that liberal economic reform was imposed on Kosovo by international officials, with privatisation the preset choice. The transfer of responsibilities for privatisation have passed from UNMIK to Kosovo's institutions, under the control of the Privatisation Agency of Kosovo (PAK). Similarly, in B&H international actors have been blamed for legitimising corruption, while in Montenegro the privatisation process led to value destruction as managers and politically connected individuals took advantage of weak institutions (Koman et al., 2015; Williams et al., 2017b).

Direct experiences of corruption, or the knowledge of its impact on family and friends, can have lasting impacts on perceptions. For all three countries, there was a wave of return migration after independence. Many members of the diaspora who had been forced to flee wanted to see their newly independent homeland succeed and to contribute to that success. However, return slowed down, with a key contributing factor to lower rates of return being corruption and the risks associated with investment. As one respondent explained, 'during that time, after independence, rules and regulations were not stable, there were a lot risks . . . the diaspora didn't perceive it as a safe place to do business' (K9), while another said that 'we had one chance to impress the first generation of diasporas but it didn't work . . . the country wasn't ready' (K6). Similarly, in both B&H and Montenegro, policy makers stated that corruption had served to dissuade returnees from investing.

As a result, institutional change has been required to improve perceptions of risk. One respondent explained that 'perceptions are very important . . . there were bad experiences following independence and we need to correct that now' (K6). Other respondents argued that key risks such as corruption have decreased, although they have not been fully tackled, leaving the impression that each country is still characterised by unstable institutional environments. As such, there is a key challenge of persuading diaspora entrepreneurs that risks have reduced and that investments have a chance to be successful. Policy makers are seeking to do this not only to attract more diaspora to return, but also to use them as role models for entrepreneurs and potential entrepreneurs within the country. This demonstration effect is important for encouraging others into economic activity (Riddle et al., 2010), as the respondents explained: 'We want our entrepreneurs to look at what the diaspora are doing and think, "I can do that, if they can do it, so can I" ' (K4); 'Our diaspora have gained lots of skills and knowledge living in Germany, Switzerland, the USA and elsewhere . . . we need them to pass that on' (K10).

One respondent stated that informal institutions need to improve, particularly with regards to perceptions of risk: 'we need to win the hearts and mind of the diaspora, especially the second generation . . . to give them something to come home for' (K2).

8.2.4. Engaging the Diaspora in Institutional Change

Improvements in institutions are clearly important for less developed economies, not simply for attracting more diaspora investment, but more generally to secure growth and slow down outward migration. In this regard, there has been some attempt to involve diaspora communities in the development of formal institutions (Riddle and Brinkerhoff, 2011; Kshetri, 2013). As Chapter 4 stated, involving the diaspora in policy making can be beneficial, as they have the potential to act as change agents in their country of origin (Riddle and Brinkerhoff, 2011; Brinkerhoff, 2016), and their expertise can be utilised for institutional improvements (Agunias and Newland, 2012).

Many of the stakeholders stated that there was a need to involve them more in political processes. One respondent stated that there was currently a lack of involvement, unlike the 'Irish and Jewish diaspora models, where there is a lot of political influence in the home country' (K3). The respondents reported that there had been 'various PR campaigns from government to show that things are improving' (K5), but that more needed to be done. Part of the attempts to do this are through improving the functioning of business networks, which are often informal and where government led schemes have not been successful: 'there have been lots of diaspora business networks but they haven't worked . . . you can't bring government and entrepreneurs together for one day and expect long-term relationships to flourish' (B2). To improve this, in Kosovo the NDS specifies that a database needs to be established to provide a central contact point to engage with the diaspora (Government of Kosovo, 2016, p. 16) so that they can be involved in decision-making. While establishing a database of diaspora was welcomed by the respondents, it was considered to be problematic; for example, one respondent commented that 'there is problem identifying the diaspora, especially the second generation . . . we need to register them so we can engage but finding them is not easy' (K8). Furthermore, a key problem was seen to be the range of formal and informal networks which seek to engage with the diaspora. One respondent said that 'we need to halt the proliferation of different networks as it makes coordination difficult : . . we need one digital network that covers all of our diaspora' (K2). Such approaches are potentially valuable given that the diaspora are often deeply engaged in digital networks and can use them to contribute to socio-economic development in their home country (Brinkerhoff, 2009).

The stakeholders stated that more needed to be done to directly involve the diaspora in institutional change. In common with other countries which have improved voting rights (Gamlen et al., 2017), there are plans to provide seats in government directly voted on by the diaspora: 'it would be good to have 4 or 5 seats in parliament to be voted on by the diaspora, so they can push for things they want to change' (K6); 'we should open consulates and embassies so people can vote directly' (B4); 'it would be good to have reserve seats like in Croatia that are voted for by the diaspora' (K12). Many of the respondents stated that the political tensions meant that changes to the structure of parliaments was difficult to introduce; however, it was considered necessary to put pressure on the government to reform institutions. As one respondent stated: 'The diaspora is always in general opposition to the government, they are always more radical than the current political discourse . . . so we need to involve them to broaden the political engagement and ideas' (K2). These views reflect the fact that the diaspora are currently not involved in or influencing institutional change. While Brinkerhoff (2016) demonstrates that diaspora entrepreneurs can play a key role in pushing for specific institutional reforms, this is currently lacking in B&H, Kosovo, and Montenegro. As two respondents stated: 'we want the diaspora to be part of institutional building . . . they haven't been so far' (B5); and 'we need to get them more involved, they can help so we need to find ways to entice them as it hasn't worked yet' (M3).

8.3. Conclusions

The chapter demonstrates that while engaging the diaspora to return home to invest can have a number of positive impacts, engagement itself is challenging. The fact that the diaspora's connectivity to the homeland weakens over time means that the need for effective, coordinated institutional change is pressing (Riddle and Brinkerhoff, 2011). Institutional improvements which enhance economic activity within the country will also enhance investment from diaspora entrepreneurs as it will reduce risk. The institutional framework in post-conflict economies may prove daunting for even experienced and well-connected diaspora investors since the environment is dynamic and changing (Nielsen and Riddle, 2010). However, while important in fostering a growing economy, general institutional improvements may not be sufficient if diaspora entrepreneurs are to be mobilised effectively for the benefit of their home country. A more proactive and coordinated programme of provision is required to educate the diaspora about institutional change and opportunities within countries, and to provide more holistic support which encompasses a wide range of business barriers. Perceptions of opportunity among diaspora entrepreneurs need to be changed. While this is a slow process, as informal institutions take time to alter (Estrin and Mickiewicz, 2011), where expectations are of a stable environment, institutions will gain legitimacy and promote activity and investment (Crawford and Ostrom, 1995). On the other hand, where expectations are of a changing environment which lacks stability and which contains inherent risks, individuals will chose to undertake entrepreneurial activity in their host countries where institutions are much more stable. Anti-corruption media campaigns are helping in this regard, but government needs to do more to demonstrate that institutions are stable and supportive. This demonstrates how policy to engage the diaspora in post-conflict economies is time-bound, with the first generation having returned despite the institutional environment not being sufficiently stable and embedded to create long-term engagement. As such, these entrepreneurs became isolated again, and there is now the challenge of assimilating first- *and* second-generation diaspora entrepreneurs to benefit the economy. Yet engaging the second generation is much harder given their weaker emotional ties to their home country. Strong connections with the homeland exist (Mollers et al., 2015), but these will decrease over time.

While remittances can play a significant role in post-conflict economies, they are not sufficient to increase entrepreneurial activity, and the flow of ideas and values is often more important (Ivlevs and King, 2012b). Yet the interviews found that the demonstration effect produced by the transfer of knowledge (Riddle and Brinkerhoff, 2011) is not being adequately harnessed. More coordinated approaches to policy can help to ensure not only that knowledge spillovers are maximised for the individuals involved (both the diaspora and those receiving investment), but also that the knowledge from this can be shared and put into practice in other contexts. Crucially, there needs to be greater involvement of the diaspora in institutional reform, as they have the potential to act as change agents (Brinkerhoff, 2016). At present, while the government is seeking to improve its relationship with the diaspora, there is a lack of real engagement and consultation related to institutional change. Akin to other areas of public policy, such as entrepreneurship and economic development, Balkan economies such as Kosovo can seek to adopt policy from elsewhere and transfer it to a new context (Xheneti and Kitching, 2011) as programmes such as TOKTEN can be replicated and learnt from. Within such policy frameworks it is important to acknowledge that there are significant political tensions in Kosovo, which means that commitment to institutional change is not guaranteed. Given the political fragmentation of the country, Kosovar Albanians are prioritised in policy discourse, and while they form the majority of the population, this means that other groups are often overlooked. In order to improve the institutional environment to mobilise greater levels of investment, it will be important that there is long-term commitment to institutional improvements which benefit all groups.

9

Conclusions

Implications for Theory, Policy, and Practice

9.1. Migration and Return

This book has focused on the diaspora who have been displaced by conflict; individuals who have moved to escape violence in their homelands or who have been displaced internally within their own country and are now returning. As such, the migrants being studied are not those who initially moved in search of opportunity. Rather, they were forced to move due to the conflict at home. Over time, they have acquired knowledge, skills, and experience in their host country, leading to increased availability of entrepreneurial and employment opportunities. Now that the situation at home has changed, with the threat of war and violence diminished, many are deciding to return home to live, work, or invest. The location of the migrants, the period they have spent abroad, as well as the conditions under which they have acquired skills and knowledge (either in employment, entrepreneurial activity, and/or education) will influence their return.

Through this focus, the book recognises the important phenomenon of return migration. Although they were forced to migrate, the individuals studied are returning to their homelands voluntarily. However, despite increasing rates of return migration, the institutional environments at home remain complicated. They are often turbulent and changing. Weak rules mean that navigating the environment is challenging, and corruption acts as an impediment on entrepreneurial activity and ambition. In addition, there is often a lack of support services to help individuals when they go back, or individuals seek to avoid the government support that is available due to mistrust.

In recognising these challenges, the book examines the motivations to return, the policy dimensions which are used to attract and support return, and the activities that these returnees undertake. These internationally mobile migrants compare the environments in their host and home countries, and make decisions based on this comparison, in relation to the activities that they will undertake. Often this means comparing the relative stability of their host

The Diaspora and Returnee Entrepreneurship. Nick Williams, Oxford University Press (2021). © Oxford University Press.
DOI: 10.1093/oso/9780190911874.003.0009

country with a greater degree of turbulence and uncertainty at home, especially in places such as post-conflict economies.

9.2. Entrepreneurship and Context

Given the increased movements of people around the world, there has been increased attention placed on the economic activity of migrants (Ram and Jones, 2008; Elo, 2016), including as entrepreneurs (Aliaga-Isla and Rialp, 2013). Migrants have been found to show a higher than average rate of entrepreneurial activity, a recurring feature across multiple historical flows of migration (Edwards et al., 2016). The international and transnational element of these migrants highlights the importance of context, as they can compare different environments and make decisions based on these comparisons.

Central to the argument of the book is the notion that institutions matter. Institutions structure the incentives to which individuals respond (North, 1990). A stable institutional environment is important for fostering entrepreneurship; while on the contrary, instability and turbulence within an economic environment will hold back entrepreneurs. Even in the most difficult environments, people find opportunities to improve their circumstances (Sautet, 2013). In challenging environments, entrepreneurial activity still takes place. In developing economies, in spite of often malfunctioning or complicated formal institutions, individual entrepreneurs still find opportunities to apply their skills, experience, and knowledge to develop ideas that satisfy market needs.

While the literature on institutions and entrepreneurship in transition economies is well established (Smallbone and Welter, 2001; Williams and Vorley, 2015), institutional development in economies which have experienced a 'path break', such as post-conflict economies, are less understood. Through a focus on post-conflict economies, this book takes forward the understanding of the complexity of place and entrepreneurial activity. Positive reforms take time, and only when the prevailing institutions foster more systemic, productive, and ambitious entrepreneurial activity will they be regarded to have been a success. Following conflict and independence, the economies of B&H, Kosovo, and Montenegro have forged new formal institutions, while informal institutions have developed in response to these changes.

The alignment of formal institutions is of critical importance to economies seeking to reform and foster higher levels of entrepreneurship. Chapter 3 demonstrated that ensuring the complementarity of formal and informal institutions is critical if entrepreneurship is to be supported. Institutions, both formal and informal, develop and change over time and the process is not linear (Brinkerhoff, 2016). Indeed, institutional frameworks are complex, and changes to formal institutions influence changes to informal institutions, and vice versa. Where the formal and informal complement each other, entrepreneurial activity will be fostered; conversely, where there is asymmetry, entrepreneurial activity will be stymied (Williams and Vorley, 2015).

Whatever the context is in which entrepreneurial activity takes place, the benefits of entrepreneurship are well established. Entrepreneurship can create employment, stimulate competition, drive forward innovation, and provide a route out of poverty. Given that entrepreneurship is generally regarded as a productive force for change in the development of modern economies, this promise also holds for post-conflict economies (Sanders and Weitzel, 2013). The post-conflict economies of B&H, Kosovo, and Montenegro have all forged new institutional frameworks. Yet as the book has shown, the perceptions of institutional change are still generally weak, meaning that there is a lack of symmetry between the formal and informal. Unless entrepreneurs and potential entrepreneurs see and experience the benefits of institutional reforms, then more productive entrepreneurship will not be secured. Individuals will avoid entrepreneurial activity when they see the risks as too great. This may not lead to a complete absence of entrepreneurship, as it always exists (Sautet, 2013). Indeed, entrepreneurial activity is taking place in each of the post-conflict economies. However, it will mean that less productive and systemic entrepreneurship, which has a real impact on economic development, is fostered. The scale of entrepreneurial activity will stay small and limited.

Independence in each of the three economies has not seen them experience the levels of economic development they were aspiring to. Unless institutional arrangements are seen to be positive, productive entrepreneurship will be stymied and growth will be reduced. Poorly devised institutional changes will serve to undermine the prospect of entrepreneurial-led growth in B&H, Kosovo, and Montenegro, and with it compound issues of political marginalization, as well as ethnic, social, and political divisions. A shift is required which sees genuine improvements in formal institutions, with stability and security of property rights the key elements, and which then leads to improved informal institutions. Only by shifting perceptions to be more positive can higher levels of productive entrepreneurship be harnessed. Where expectations are of a stable environment, institutions will gain legitimacy and enhance compliance (Crawford and Ostrom, 1995). On the contrary, where expectations are of a changing environment which lacks stability, individuals may seek to circumvent rules or may not risk undertaking entrepreneurial activity. This requires policy makers to tackle corruption so that levels of trust can increase. Improvements in regulations may prove temporary as social values will translate to different policy areas. In economies with weak or negative perceptions and expectations, informal institutions will take time to change (Winiecki, 2001; Estrin and Mickiewicz, 2011) but can be targeted through media campaigns, education, and utilization of role models (Hindle and Klyver, 2007).

Linked to this, there is a need to develop the ambition and capabilities of entrepreneurs in order to foster more productive entrepreneurship, which will in turn increase the complementarity of formal and informal institutions. This focus on developing and embedding institutions is particularly critical given the geopolitical challenges facing each of the three countries, as further political marginalization and tensions will undoubtedly constrain opportunities for entrepreneurship and growth.

9.3. Returnee Entrepreneurs: Caught Between Isolation and Assimilation

Institutions obviously matter for indigenous entrepreneurs who live and work within national borders; yet they are equally important for those who have moved away and are considering return. The book has focused on the role of returnee entrepreneurs, defined as individuals who have moved away from their home country and have lived as part of the diaspora, and have later returned home to live, invest, or both. These returnees represent a distinct form of entrepreneurs, as they are exposed to both home and host country institutional environments (Qin and Estrin, 2015; Lin et al., 2018), and differential experiences in terms of education, employment, and culture. Despite seeing increased attention in the entrepreneurship literature, there is still much that is unknown regarding returnees. Success stories of return, such as Silicon Valley entrepreneurs connecting to their homelands and increased return to fast-growing China (Lin et al., 2018), are emerging in the research, although relatively little is known regarding turbulent environments.

This book has provided a platform for further understanding the important phenomenon of return migration and entrepreneurship through a focus on environments that are turbulent and complex. This book furthers understanding of returnees by showing that those who move abroad can often be caught between isolation and assimilation. Many potential investors are discouraged by unstable institutional environments. They are reluctant to return despite having an emotional connection to home. Chapter 5 showed that business experience can have a negative relationship on the probability to return.

The more time individuals spend in the host country, the more they become embedded within that context. Years of living abroad increase isolation from the homeland.

Nevertheless, the book also shows that individuals are returning, even though there are very real challenges associated with operating in the homeland. Following independence in each of the countries studied, new waves of return were seen. Many of the returnees found the institutional environment unready for investment and left again. Other members of the diaspora have returned later, when they perceived that the institutional environment had sufficiently improved. This does not mean that it compares favourably with their host country environment, but that the balance of risks and rewards suggests that activity can take place without the fear of losing everything. Yet although many of these have returned and have launched successful businesses, they do not fully assimilate in their home economies. They avoid government engagement activities as they mistrust politicians' intentions and will often only work with networks of family and friends. They will also often maintain investments in their host country as a way of diversifying their business portfolio and insuring themselves against the risks in the homeland.

In this way, when the diaspora return to complex environments, they are not acting as change agents (Riddle and Brinkerhoff, 2011; Kshetri, 2013). They are not acting as institutional entrepreneurs who help to transform an institution. They key reason for this is the lack of trust in institutions. Chapter 5 showed that the diaspora's intentions to return are affected by a lack of trust in the institutional setting. Members of the diaspora who lack trust in institutions and have high risk perceptions are less likely to have entrepreneurial intentions for the homeland. Furthermore, Chapter 7 showed differences in trust between the internally displaced and migrants who moved abroad. External migrants have lower trust in institutions in comparison to internal migrants, which can be explained by their exposure to the institutional environment in their host country.

9.4. The Embeddedness of Entrepreneurs across Borders

Differences in institutional trust and the notion of *isolation and assimilation* demonstrate that embeddedness across borders has differential impacts on the individual. This highlights that entrepreneurship is a socialised process (Drakopolou Dodd and Anderson, 2007) and that there is a relationship between the entrepreneurial self and society (Jack and Anderson, 2002).

Embeddedness explains how context and community influence perceived possibilities in particular situations (Welter, 2011) and acts to either enable or constrain entrepreneurial activity (Johnstone and Lionais, 2004).

Figure 9.1 demonstrates how individuals become embedded in the host country by adapting to their new context, developing international experience and new networks. These individuals choose to return to their homeland to undertake entrepreneurial activity and benefit from embeddedness there, drawing on previous networks and their understanding of the local context. For those returning to fast-growing economies (Home Country Type A in Figure 9.1), opportunities will be realised to achieve financial gains. While such economies can also be turbulent, they have greater levels of opportunity associated with economic expansion. In more challenging and turbulent economies (Home Country Type B), where growth is low and constrained, the opportunity for returns to self can be a more prevalent factor.

The book has highlighted that the prevalent research on returnees focuses on realising profit opportunities in fast-growing dynamic economies (see, for example, Qin et al., 2017). Entrepreneurs who return can fill entrepreneurial gaps in terms of innovation and technological knowledge (Li et al., 2012; Lin et al., 2018). However, by examining returnee entrepreneurship to unstable economies, the book shows that gains from such innovation and technology may be reduced. Indeed, the book finds that international experience can act to temper the potential for entrepreneurial activity at home. This reflects how the knowledge gained abroad, often working as an employee in a large-scale business, is not directly replicable at home. The kinds of businesses that many of the diaspora worked for do not exist at home. While Qin et al. (2017)

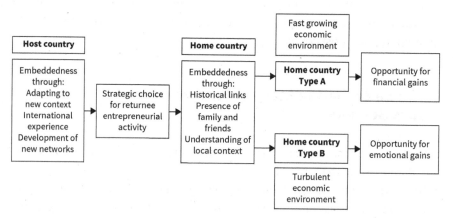

Figure 9.1 Embeddedness of returnee entrepreneurs across borders.

demonstrate that returnees can use their experience at home, the role of international experience is reduced in turbulent environments.

In applying the theory of embeddedness to internationally mobile returnee entrepreneurs, the book takes forward research on the returns associated with entrepreneurial activity. Embeddedness strengthens an individual's ties to an environment (Jack and Anderson, 2002), and this can be used to derive benefits in the host country which can then be drawn upon when returning home. Returnee entrepreneurs utilise their relational embeddedness through connections with family and friends to overcome many of the challenges associated with transnational activity and turbulent environments.

Investments in family and friends demonstrate how entrepreneurial behaviour is not simply concerned with economic self-interest and show how entrepreneurs can act based on their concern for 'known others'; and further to this, they can act out of concern for 'unknown others' (Gruber and MacMillan, 2017). However, the book goes beyond such benevolence by examining how the investments are motivated by consideration of the self rather than wider society. Assisting 'known others' through strategic investments is a method for maximising emotional satisfaction. In this sense, embeddedness enables understanding of how group connections shape actions (Portes and Sensenbrenner, 1993). Within social structures, entrepreneurs can create and extract value (Hansen, 1995). Returnee entrepreneurs invest in family and friends and thus access 'socialised reservoirs' of knowledge, experiences, and other localised resources (Jack et al., 2008). Connections to family and friends enable embeddedness through shared values, within-group trust, historical reciprocity, and bounded solidarity, which are privileged aspects of local belonging (Anderson et al., 2012).

However, this means that rather than focusing on potentially innovative and/or profitable opportunities, many of the diaspora who return to their homeland to invest will be concerned with social outcomes. Returnees receive emotional gains by investing in activities which impact on society, rather than necessarily seeking profits. Altruistic behaviour can be undertaken with the intention to benefit other people, but the emotional returns to self are often overlooked. In this, returnee entrepreneurs differ from (more) traditional entrepreneurs as they seek returns beyond financial gains. At the same time, returnee entrepreneurs face different costs and risks compared to traditional entrepreneurs. These include the social pressure of being a native of the home country, and political pressures due to the unstable institutional environment. As such, returnee entrepreneurs can invest in the expectation of a 'warm glow' (Arrow, 1972).

Consideration of embeddedness in returnee entrepreneurship is important given that returnee entrepreneurs are often internationally experienced, and are able to traverse and compare the relative pay-offs of different economic contexts. Drawing on embeddedness offers a mechanism for understanding the relationship between individuals and place, and how this engagement shapes the entrepreneur's sense of self. In synthesising and applying this conceptual insight, we provide a contextually sensitive view of the entrepreneur's motivation when investing at home. This book moves forward the embeddedness perspective by demonstrating the importance of gaining returns to self in fostering entrepreneurial action. Pride in action is achieved through working in communities where the returnees have an emotional connection, with returnee entrepreneurs not necessarily seeking to maximise profits. Instead, they utilise their embeddedness in the home country to derive emotional gains.

9.5. Institutional Change and the Role of Policy

The book has emphasised the importance of institutions in fostering entrepreneurship, and how policy makers are seeking to change institutions to make return investment more attractive. The institutional environment is a key element of any analysis of migrant, immigrant, or ethnic entrepreneurship (Ram et al., 2016), and as the book has made clear, institutional reform is a critical aspect of engagement and mobilisation of diaspora entrepreneurs. Tackling negative perceptions is crucial if investment is to be secured.

Institutional improvements which enhance economic activity within the country will also enhance investment from the diaspora. Enhancements to institutions reduce risk and improve perceptions. As such, a key policy recommendation of the book is on the face of it very simple: improve the institutional environment. This means securing property rights, making it easy to start a business and for the entrepreneur to retain profits. Certainly, these reforms are necessary if external investors, including the diaspora, are to see the institutional environment as supportive of entrepreneurship. All three economies studied in this book have a long way to go to improve their institutions, and improvements are necessary to secure future growth.

However, when considering return, general institutional improvements may not be sufficient if the diaspora are to be mobilised effectively for the benefit of their home country.

Given the economic, social, and demographic challenges in each of these post-conflict economies, policy focused on returnees has the potential to contribute significantly to development, especially given that the diaspora may be driven to invest through emotional ties and a 'country-of-origin bias' (Nielsen and Riddle, 2010). If complex environments such as the Balkan economies are to overcome the numerous economic and social challenges facing them, then increased diaspora investment and involvement in policy making is required.

As the majority of policies to promote investment and entrepreneurship only see impacts in the long term, coordinated efforts must be maintained over the long term. At the same time, the fact that the connectivity of the diaspora to their homeland weakens over time means that there is a pressing need for effective, coordinated policy now (Riddle and Brinkerhoff, 2011). Chapter 4 showed that while policy makers were making numerous efforts to try to engage the diaspora to return, the impact of this was limited. A more proactive and coordinated programme of provision and advice is required to educate the diaspora about policy developments and opportunities within countries, and to provide more holistic support which encompasses a wide range of business barriers.

Coordinated policy has a role to play to ensure that investment and the transfer of knowledge is maximised. Spillovers from the transfer of knowledge have wide-ranging benefits, including introducing new ways of working to the homeland, and adding skills and knowledge of how to undertake entrepreneurial activity. Critically, governments need to make attempts to involve the diaspora in policy making. While many governments are keen to improve their relationships with the diaspora, policy has not always been effective. The book has found evidence of scepticism regarding the motives of policy making, with the diaspora avoiding aspects such as government-created digital registries out of fear for how their contact details will be used. There has been some success with registries created by NGOs, such as Germin in Kosovo; however, these remain largely outside of government engagement. There is also scepticism related to corruption among politicians, with the diaspora unwilling to take support from government for fear that they may then be subject to pressures. Giving the diaspora voting rights may be a valuable PR exercise that should be pursued by policy makers, although it is difficult to see that this would lead to genuine improvements in government action.

Governments in turbulent and complex economies should seek to learn more from countries which have successfully engaged the diaspora, for example China's programmes to attract high-skilled workers home. Schemes such as TOKTEN, which link the diaspora with employment and entrepreneurial opportunities at home, can also be useful. Such schemes can be developed to meet specific economic needs at home, for example by linking the skilled diaspora to opportunities which would alleviate demographic pressures at home, such as creating training programmes for young people, or allowing placements in successful companies so that they can develop skills.

These policy developments must also recognise that engaging the diaspora in return is not always 'win-win' (Pellerin and Mullings, 2013) and there are distinct challenges for policy makers in ensuring that it impacts positively on economic development. Returnees may crowd out activity in the homeland, or engage in activity which contributes little to economic development. Chapter 8 showed that, despite their keenness to engage with the diaspora, there was some scepticism among policy makers regarding the skills that are being brought. Policy makers said that many among the diaspora had done low-skilled work or entrepreneurial activity in their host country and that these skills would add little to the homeland. As such, there is a need to consider the skills of the returnees when prioritising policy. If the highly skilled can be attracted home, there is greater potential productive entrepreneurship which contributes to growth. Yet these programmes depend largely on the local partnerships available. Consequently, policy makers must look to partner entrepreneurs at home with the skills of returnees, so that gaps can be filled in terms of knowledge and experience. However, the success of programmes such as these can only happen if they are combined with institutional change which provides stability and security, so that the risks associated with entrepreneurship are reduced. Only then can trust in the institutional framework be enhanced, which will lead to higher levels of investment.

9.6. Closing Remarks

As global migration continues to grow, the role of returnees are becoming an ever more important aspect of entrepreneurship research. In bringing together the literature on the diaspora and return, this book has demonstrated how they can contribute through remittances, skills and knowledge transfer, and direct investment. The role of the returnee should not be underestimated. Yet if their productive potential is to be harnessed, countries with challenging institutional environments need to do more to 'fix' the challenges that returnees face. The focus needs to be on clear rules and regulations, tackling corruption, and allowing the rewards associated with the activity to be retained by the entrepreneur. Clearly, institutional change is a long-term endeavour, and returnees can have a role in changing institutions (Brinkerhoff, 2016). Governments must do more to show positive change. This means making real and effective institutional changes, which benefit entrepreneurs at home and those thinking of return. In addition, reforms need to be communicated so that change is demonstrated. This will lead to greater trust in policy and change. The book has demonstrated that the lack of real assimilation of the diaspora in the homelands, characterised by complexity, represents a key challenge for ensuring real economic impacts. As governments around the world seek to gain advantages from return migration, countries with complex environments and low growth have huge opportunities if they can position themselves to receive returnee skills, knowledge, and experience. Growth will be improved, enriching the lives of people in the homeland, helping to insure them against future downturns, and creating more opportunities to advance trade within and outside borders. The diaspora offers great potential. As lessons from more dynamic economies show, the diaspora are no longer isolated. Effective policies and attractive institutional environments are bringing them home. Yet in complex economies the diaspora are not assimilated, despite the desire of many to contribute to their homeland due to an emotional connection. As such, the diaspora of these economies represent an underutilised and potentially very important resource. If their skills, knowledge, and experience can be harnessed, then the homeland can experience increased growth. This requires commitment from all stakeholders involved in institutional change, and it is to be hoped that through the lessons contained within this book and by drawing on relevant successful policy changes elsewhere, more returnee investment can be secured. There is no 'magic bullet' in terms of policy change—no single change that will ignite the spark of greater levels of productive entrepreneurship among the returning diaspora. Rather, concerted efforts over time are required, with commitment to effective reform the surest way to ensure that the diaspora see opportunities to return.

References

Acs, Z. J. (2006) How is entrepreneurship good for economic growth? *Innovations* 1(1), 97–107.

Acs, Z. J., Braunerhjelm, P., Audretsch, D. B., and Carlsson, B. (2009) The knowledge spillover theory of entrepreneurship. *Small Business Economics* 32(1), 15–30.

Acs, Z. J., Desai, S., and Hessels, J. (2008) Entrepreneurship, economic development and institutions. *Small Business Economics* 31, 219–234.

Acs, Z. J., and Plummer, L. A. (2005) Penetrating the knowledge filter in regional economies. *The Annals of Regional Science* 39(3), 439–456.

Acemoglu, D., and Robinson, J. A. (2012) *Why nations fail: The origins of power, prosperity and poverty*. Profile Books, London.

Adamson, F. B. (2006) Crossing borders: International migration and national security. *International Security* 31(1), 165–199.

Adler, P., and Kwon, S. W. (2002) Social capital: Prospects for a new concept. *Academy of Management Review* 27(1), 17–40.

Agunias, D. R., and Newland, K. (2012) *Developing a roadmap for engaging diasporas for development: A handbook for policy makers and practitioners in home and host countries*. International Organization for Migration, Geneva.

Ahlstrom, D., and Bruton, G. D. (2010) *International management: Strategy and culture in the emerging world*. South-Western, Mason, OH.

Aidis, R., and Adachi, Y. (2007) Russia: Firm entry and survival barriers. *Economic Systems* 31, 391–411.

Aidis, R., Estrin, S., and Mickiewicz, T. (2008) Institutions and entrepreneurship development in Russia: A comparative perspective. *Journal of Business Venturing* 23(6), 656–672.

Al-Laham, A., and Souitaris, V. (2008) Network embeddedness and new venture internalization: Analyzing international linkages in the German biotech industry. *Journal of Business Venturing* 23, 567–586.

Aldrich, H., and Zimmer, C. (1986) Entrepreneurship through social networks. In D. Sexton and R. Smilor (eds.), *The art and science of entrepreneurship*. Ballinger, Cambridge, MA, pp. 3–24.

Aliaga-Isla, R., and Rialp, A. (2013) Systematic review of immigrant entrepreneurship literature: Previous findings and ways forward. *Entrepreneurship & Regional Development* 25, 819–844.

Anderson, A. R., Drakopoulou Dodd, S., and Jack, S. (2010) Network practices and entrepreneurial growth. *Scandinavian Journal of Management* 26(2), 121–133.

Anderson, A. R., Drakopoulou Dodd, S., and Jack, S. (2012) Entrepreneurship as connecting: Some implications for theorising and practice. *Management Decision* 50, 958–971.

Andersson, M., and Ejermo, O. (2005) How does accessibility to knowledge sources affect the innovativeness of corporations? Evidence from Sweden. *Annals of Regional Science* 39, 741–765.

Andersson, M., and Karlsson, C. (2007) Knowledge in regional economic growth: The role of knowledge accessibility. *Industry and Innovation* 14(2), 129–149.

Anokhin, S., and Schulze, W. S. (2009) Entrepreneurship, innovation and corruption. *Journal of Business Venturing* 24, 465–476.

Armakolas, I. (2011) The paradox of Tuzla City: Explaining non-nationalist local politics during the Bosnian war. *Europe-Asia Studies* 63(2), 229–261.

Arrow, K. J. (1972) Gifts and exchanges. *Philosophy and Public Affairs* 1(1), 343–362.

Atherton, A. (2006) Should government be stimulating start-ups? An assessment of the scope for public intervention in new venture formation. *Environment and Planning C: Government and Policy* 24(1), 21–36.

Audretsch, D. B. (2003) Entrepreneurship policy and the strategic management of places. In D. M. Hart (ed.), *The emergence of entrepreneurship policy: Governance, start-ups and growth in the U.S. knowledge economy*. Cambridge University Press, Cambridge, pp. 20–38.

Audretsch, D. B. (2007) Entrepreneurship capital and economic growth. *Oxford Review of Economic Policy* 23(1), 63–78.

Audretsch, D. B., and Fritsch, M. (2002) Growth regimes over time and space. *Regional Studies* 36(2), 113–124.

Audretsch, D. B., Grilo, I., and Thurik, A. R. (2007) Explaining entrepreneurship and the role of policy: A framework. In D. B. Audretsch et al. (eds.), *The handbook of research on entrepreneurship policy*. Edward Elgar, Cheltenham, UK, and Northampton, MA, pp. 1–17.

Audretsch, D. B., and Keilbach, M. (2004) Entrepreneurship and regional growth: An evolutionary interpretation. *Journal of Evolutionary Economics* 14(5), 605–616.

Audretsch, D. B., and Keilbach, M. (2005) Entrepreneurship capital and regional growth. *The Annals of Regional Science* 39(3), 457–469.

Audretsch, D. B., Keilbach, M., and Lehmann, E. (2006) *Entrepreneurship and economic growth*. Oxford University Press, Oxford.

Autio, E. (2017) Strategic entrepreneurial internationalization: A normative framework. *Strategic Entrepreneurship Journal* 11(3), 211–227.

Axelrod, R. (1985) *The evolution of cooperation*. Basic Books, New York.

Bagwell, S. (2015) Transnational entrepreneurship amongst Vietnamese businesses in London. *Journal of Ethnic and Migration Studies* 41(2), 329–349.

Bakewell, O. (2008) In search of the diasporas within Africa. *African Diaspora* 1(1), 5–27.

Baron, R. A. (2008) The role of affect in the entrepreneurial process. *Academy of Management Review* 33(2), 328–340.

Bathelt, H., Malmberg, A., and Maskell, P. (2004) Clusters and knowledge: Local buzz, global pipelines and the process of knowledge creation. *Progress in Human Geography* 28(1), 31–56.

Baumol, W. J. (1990) Entrepreneurship: Productive, unproductive and destructive. *Journal of Political Economy* 98(5), 892–921.

Baycan-Levent, T., and Nijkamp, P. (2009) Characteristics of migrant entrepreneurship in Europe. *Entrepreneurship and Regional Development* 21(4), 375–397.

Becker, G. S. (1996) *Accounting for tastes*. Harvard University Press, Cambridge, MA.

Belloni, R., and Strazzari, F. (2014) Corruption in post-conflict Bosnia-Herzegovina and Kosovo: A deal among friends. *Third World Quarterly* 35(5), 855–871.

Benz, M. (2005) Not for the profit, but for the satisfaction? Evidence on worker well-being in non-profit firms. *Kyklos* 58(2), 155–176.

Benz, M. (2009) Entrepreneurship as a non-profit seeking activity. *International Entrepreneurship and Management Journal* 5(1), 23–44.

Bieber, F. (2003) *Montenegro in transition: Problems of identity and statehood*. Nomos, Baden-Baden.

Bieber, F. (2010) *Post-war Bosnia: Ethnicity, inequality and public sector governance*. Palgrave MacMillan, London.

Bird, M., and Wennberg, K. (2016) Why family matters: The impact of family resources on immigrant entrepreneurs' exit from entrepreneurship. *Journal of Business Venturing* 31, 687–704.

Blackburn, R. A., and Ram, M. (2006) Fix or fixation? The contributions and limitations of entrepreneurship and small firms to combating social exclusion. *Entrepreneurship and Regional Development* 18(1), 73–89.

Boettke, P., and Coyne, C. (2003) Entrepreneurship and economic development: Cause or consequence. In R. Koppl (ed.), *Austrian economics and entrepreneurial studies*. Elsevier, Oxford, pp. 67–88.

Bowey, J. L., and Easton, G. (2007) Entrepreneurial social capital unplugged: An activity-based analysis. *International Small Business Journal* 25, 273–306.

Braunerhjelm, P., Acs, Z. J., Audretsch, D. B., and Carlsson, B. (2009) The missing link: Knowledge diffusion and entrepreneurship in endogenous growth. *Small Business Economics* 34(2), 105–125.

Brinkerhoff, J. (2009) *Digital diasporas: Identity and transnational engagement*. Cambridge University Press, Cambridge.

Brinkerhoff, J. (2011) Diasporas and conflict societies: Conflict entrepreneurs, competing interests or contributors to stability and development. *Conflict, Security and Development* 11(2), 115–143.

Brinkerhoff, J. (2012) Creating an enabling environment for diaspora's participation in home-land development. *International Migration* 50(1), 75–95.

Brinkerhoff, J. (2016) *Institutional reform and diaspora entrepreneurs: The in-between advantage*. Oxford University Press, Oxford.

Brinkerhoff, J. (2017) Diaspora policy in weakly governed arenas and the benefits of multi-polar engagement: Lessons from the Coptic Orthodox Church in Egypt. *Journal of Ethnic and Migration Studies* 45(4), 561–576.

Bruck, T., Naude, W., and Verwimp, P. (2013) Business under fire: Entrepreneurship and violent conflict in developing countries. *Journal of Conflict Resolution* 57(1), 3–19.

Bruton, G. D., Ahlstrom, D., and Li, H. L. (2010) Institutional theory and entrepreneurship: Where are we now and where do we need to move in the future? *Entrepreneurship Theory and Practice* 34, 421–440.

Bullough, A., Renko, M., and Myatt, T. (2014) Danger zone entrepreneurs: The importance of resilience and self-efficacy for entrepreneurial intentions. *Entrepreneurship Theory and Practice* 38(3), 473–499.

Busenitz, L. W, Gomez, C., and Spencer, J. W. (2000) Country institutional profiles: Unlocking entrepreneurial phenomena. *Academy of Management Journal* 43(5), 994–1003.

Bylund, P., and McCaffrey, M. (2017) A theory of entrepreneurship and institutional uncertainty. *Journal of Business Venturing* 32, 461–475.

Byrne, O., and Shepherd, D. (2015) Different strokes for different folks: Entrepreneurial narratives of emotion, cognition and making sense of business failure. *Entrepreneurship Theory and Practice* 39(2), 375–405.

Cantillon, R. (1931) *Essai sur la nature du commerce en general*. MacMillan, London.

Cardon, M., Foo, M.-D., Shepherd, D., and Wiklund, J. (2012) Exploring the heart: Entrepreneurial emotion is a hot topic. *Entrepreneurship Theory and Practice* 36(1), 1–10.

Chandler, A. (1977) *The visible hand: The managerial revolution in American business*. Belknap Press, Cambridge, MA.

Cheung, C. W. M., and Kwong, C. (2017) Path-and place-dependence of entrepreneurial ventures at times of war and conflict. *International Small Business Journal* 35(8), 903–927.

Clemens, M. A., Özden, Ç., and Rapoport, H. (2014) Migration and development research is moving far beyond remittances. *World Development* 64, 121–124.

Coleman, J. S. (1990) *Foundations of social theory*. Harvard University Press, Cambridge, MA.

Coleman, J. S. (2000) Social capital in the creation of human capital. In P. Dasgupta and I. Serageldin (eds.), *Social capital: A multifaceted perspective*. World Bank, Washington, DC.

Collier, P. (2015) *Exodus: How migration is changing our world*. Oxford University Press, Oxford.

Collier, P., and Duponchel, M. (2013) The economic legacy of civil war: Firm-level evidence from Sierra Leone. *Journal of Conflict Resolution* 57(1), 65–88.

Cowen, T., and Coyne, C. (2005) Postwar reconstruction: Some insights from public choice and institutional economics. *Constitutional Political Economy* 16(1), 31–48.

Crawford, S. E., and Ostrom, E. (1995) A grammar of institutions. *The American Political Science Review* 89(1), 582–600.

Dacin, M. T., Ventresca, M. J., and Beal, B. D. (1999) The embeddedness of organisations: Dialogue and directions. *Journal of Management* 25(3), 317–353.

De Haas, H. (2010) Migration and development: A theoretical perspective. *International Migration Review* 44, 227–264.

Demmers, J. (2007) New wars and diasporas: Suggestions for research and policy. *Journal of Peace and Conflict* 11(1), 1–26.

Desai, S., Acs, Z., and Weitzel, U. (2013) A model of destructive entrepreneurship: Insight on conflict and post-conflict recovery. *Journal of Conflict Resolution* 57(1), 20–40.

Dickinson, J. (2017) The political geographies of diaspora strategies: Rethinking the 'sending state'. *Geography Compass*, doi: 10.1111/gec3.12305

DiMaggio, P. J., and Powell, W. (1983) The iron cage revisited: Institutional isomorphism and collective rationality in organizational fields. *American Sociological Review* 48(1), 147–160.

Doern, R., and Goss, D. (2013) The role of negative emotions in the social processes of entrepreneurship: Power rituals and shame-related appeasement behaviours. *Entrepreneurship Theory and Practice* 38(4), 863–890.

Douhan, R., Eliasson, G., and Henrekson, M. (2007) Israel M. Kirzner: An outstanding Austrian contributor to the economics of entrepreneurship. *Small Business Economics* 29(1–2), 213–223.

Drakic, M., Sautet, F., and McKenzie, K. (2007) *Montenegro: The challenges of a newborn state*. Mercatus Center, Fairfax, VA.

Drakopolou Dodd, S., and Anderson, A., (2007) Mumpsimus and mything of the individualistic entrepreneur. *International Small Business Journal* 25(4), 341–360.

Drori, I., Honig, B., and Wright, M. (2009) Transnational entrepreneurship: An emergent field of study. *Entrepreneurship Theory and Practice* 33(5), 1001–1022.

Dustmann, and Kirchkamp. (2002). The optimal migration duration and activity choice after remigration. *Journal of Development Economics* 67(2), 351–372.

Eastmond, M. (2006) Transnational returns and reconstruction in post-war Bosnia and Herzegovina 44(3), 141–166.

Edwards, P., Ram, M., Jones, T., and Doldor, S. (2016) New migrant businesses and their workers: Developing, but not transforming, the ethnic economy. *Ethnic and Racial Studies* 39(9), 1587–1617.

Efendic, A., Babic, B., and Rebmann, A. (2014) *Diaspora and development in Bosnia and Herzegovina*. Embassy of Switzerland in Bosnia and Herzegovina, Sarajevo.

Efendic, A., Mickiewicz, T., and Rebmann, A. (2015) Growth aspiration and social capital: Young firms in a post-conflict environment. *International Small Business Journal* 33(5), 537–561.

Efendic, A., Pugh, G., and Adnett, N. (2011) Confidence in formal institutions and reliance on informal institutions: An empirical investigation using survey data. *Economics of Transition* 19(3), 521–540.

Elo, M. (2016) Typology of diaspora entrepreneurship: Case studies in Uzbekistan. *Journal of International Entrepreneurship* 14, 121–155.

Elo, M., and Riddle, L. (2016) *Diaspora business*. Interdisciplinary Press, Oxford.

Estrin, S., and Mickiewicz, T. (2011) Entrepreneurship in transition economies: The role of institutions and generational change. In M. Minniti (ed.), *The dynamics of entrepreneurship*. Oxford University Press, Oxford.

Estrin, S., Mickiewicz, T., and Stephan, U. (2016) Human capital in social and commercial entrepreneurship. *Journal of Business Venturing* 31(4), 449–467.

Estrin, S., and Prevezer, M. (2011) The role of informal institutions in corporate governance: Brazil, Russia, India, and China compared. *Asia Pacific Journal of Management* 28(1), 41–67.

European Commission. (2012) *Social impact of emigration and rural-urban migration in Central and Eastern Europe: Final country report Montenegro.* European Commission, Brussels.

European Commission. (2014) *Instrument for pre-accession assistance (IPA II) indicative strategy paper for Montenegro, 2014–2020.* European Commission, Brussels.

Faist, T. (2008) Migrants as transnational development agents: An inquiry into the newest round of the migration-development nexus. *Population, Space and Place* 14(1), 21–42.

Federal Ministry for Economic Cooperation and Development. (2012) *Analysis of migration strategies in selected countries.* FMECD, Berlin.

Feldman, M. P. (2001) The entrepreneurial event revisited: Firm formation in a regional context. *Industrial and Corporate Change* 10(4), 861–891.

Filatotchev, I., Liu, X., Buck, T., and Wright, M. (2009) The export orientation and export performances of high-technology SMEs in emerging markets: The effects of knowledge transfer by returnee entrepreneurs. *Journal of International Business Studies* 40(6), 1005–1021.

Foo, M.-D. (2011) Emotions and entrepreneurial opportunity evaluation. *Entrepreneurship Theory and Practice* 35(2), 375–393.

Frederking, L. C. (2004) A cross-national study of culture, organization and entrepreneurship in three neighbourhoods. *Entrepreneurship and Regional Development* 16(3), 197–215.

Galbraith, J. K. (1956) *American capitalism: The concept of countervailing power.* Houghton Mifflin, Boston.

Gamlen, A. (2006) *Diaspora engagement policies: What are they and what kinds of states use them?* WP-06-32. Centre on Migration, Policy, and Society, Oxford.

Gamlen, A. (2014) Diaspora institutions and diaspora governance. *International Migration Review* 48(1), 180–217.

Gamlen, A., Cumming, M. E., and Vaaler, P. M. (2017) Explaining the rise of diaspora institutions. *Journal of Ethnic and Migration Studies*, doi: 10.1080/1369183X.2017.1409163

Gillespie, K., Riddle, L., Sayre, E., and Sturges, D. (1999) Diaspora interest in homeland investment. *Journal of International Business Studies* 30(3), 623–634.

Gillespie, K., Sayre, E., and Riddle, L. (2001) Palestinian interest in homeland investment. *Middle East Journal* 55(2), 237–255.

Glenny, M. (1996) *The fall of Yugoslavia.* Penguin, London.

Global Entrepreneurship Monitor. (2015) *2014 Georgia report.* GEM, London.

Global Entrepreneurship Monitor. (2018) *GEM Global Entrepreneurship Monitor executive report.* GEM, London.

Government of Kosovo. (2015) *Programme of the government of the Republic of Kosovo 2015–2018.* Government of Kosovo, Pristina.

Government of Kosovo. (2016) *National Development Strategy 2016–2021.* Government of Kosovo, Pristina.

Government of Montenegro. (2014) *Analytical study of Montenegrin diaspora.* Government of Montenegro, Podgorica.

Government of Montenegro. (2016) *Action plan implementation strategy for cooperation with emigrants.* Government of Montenegro, Podgorica.

Granovetter, M. (1973) The strength of weak ties. *American Journal of Sociology* 78(6), 1360–1380.

Granovetter, M. (1985) Economic action and social structure: The problem of embeddedness. *The American Journal of Sociology* 91(3), 481–510.

Granovetter, M. (1992) Problems of explanation in economic sociology. In N. Nohria and R. Eccles (eds.), *Networks and organizations: Structure, form, and action.* Harvard Business School Press, Boston, pp. 25–56.

Greenspan, A., and Wooldridge, A. (2018) *Capitalism in America: A history.* Penguin, London.

Gruber, M., and MacMillan, I. C. (2017) Entrepreneurial behaviour: A reconceptualization and extension based on identity theory. *Strategic Entrepreneurship Journal* 11(3), 271–286.

Gurtoo, A., and Williams, C. C. (2009) Entrepreneurship and the informal sector: Some lessons from India. *International Journal of Entrepreneurship and Innovation* 10(1), 55–62.

Guseva, A. (2007) Friends and foes: Informal networks in the Soviet Union. *East European Quarterly* 41(1), 2–9.

Halilovich, H. (2012) Trans-local communities in the age of transnationalism: Bosnians in diaspora. *International Migration* 50(1), 162–178.

Hamdouch, B., and Wahba, J. (2015) Return migration and entrepreneurship in Morocco. *Middle East Development Journal* 7(2), 129–148.

Hansen, E. L. (1995) Entrepreneurial network and new organization growth. *Entrepreneurship Theory and Practice* 19(4), 7–19.

Hashi, I., and Krasniqi, B. A. (2011) Entrepreneurship and SME growth: Evidence from advanced and laggard transition economies. *International Journal of Entrepreneurial Behavior & Research* 17(5), 456–487.

Hausmann, R., and Nedelkoska, L. (2018) Welcome home in a crisis: Effects of return migration on the non-migrants' wages and employment. *European Economic Review* 101, 101–132.

Hayek, F. A. (1945) The use of knowledge in society. *American Economic Review* 35(51), 9–30.

Hayton, J. C., George, G., and Zahra, S. A. (2002) National culture and entrepreneurship: A review of behavioural research. *Entrepreneurship: Theory and Practice* 26(4), 33–52.

Hébert, R. F., and Link, A. N. (1989) In search of the meaning of entrepreneurship. *Small Business Economics* 1(1), 39–49.

Hechavarria, D. M., and Reynolds, P. D. (2009) Cultural norms and business start-ups: The impact of national values on opportunity and necessity entrepreneurs. *International Entrepreneurship and Management Journal* 5(4), 417–437.

Henrekson, M. (2007) Entrepreneurship and institutions. *Comparative Labour Law and Policy Journal* 28(3), 717–742.

Hindle, K., and Klyver, K. (2007) Exploring the relationship between media coverage and participation in entrepreneurship: Initial global evidence and research implications. *International Entrepreneurship and Management Journal* 3(2), 217–242.

Ho, E. L. E. (2011) 'Claiming' the diaspora: Elite mobility, sending state strategies and the spatialities of citizenship. *Progress in Human Geography* 35(6), 757–772.

Hockenos, P. (2003) *Homeland calling: Exile patriotism and the Balkan wars.* Cornell University Press, Ithaca, NY.

Hofstede, G. (1991) *Cultures and organizations: Software of the mind.* McGraw-Hill, London.

Holcombe, R. G. (2007) Entrepreneurship and economic growth. In B. Powell (ed.), *Making poor nations rich: Entrepreneurship and the process of economic development.* Stanford University Press, Stanford, CA.

Holtz-Eakin, D. (2000) Public policy toward entrepreneurship. *Small Business Economics* 15(4), 283–291.

Hoxha, D. (2009) Barriers to doing business in Kosova: An institutional approach. *International Journal on Entrepreneurship and Small Business* 8(2), 186–199.

Huggins, R., and Williams, N. (2009) Enterprise and public policy: A review of Labour government intervention in the United Kingdom. *Environment and Planning C: Government and Policy* 27(1), 19–41.

Huggins, R., and Williams, N. (2011) Entrepreneurship and regional competitiveness: The role and progression of policy. *Entrepreneurship and Regional Development* 23(9–10), 907–932.

International Labour Organization. (2001) *Policy responses to the international mobility of skilled labour.* ILO, Geneva.

Ivlevs, A., and King, R. M. (2012a) Kosovo: Winning its independence but losing its people? Recent evidence on emigration intentions and preparedness to migrate. *International Migration* 53(5), 84–103.

Ivlevs, A., and King, R. M. (2012b) Does more schooling make you run for the border? Evidence from post-independence Kosovo. *The Journal of Development Studies* 48(8), 1108–1120.

Jack, S. L. (2005) The role, use and activation of strong and weak network ties: A qualitative analysis. *Journal of Management Studies* 42, 1233–1259.

Jack, S. L., and Anderson, A. R. (2002) The effects of embeddedness on the entrepreneurial process. *Journal of Business Venturing* 17(5), 467–487.

Jack, S. L., Drakopoulou Dodd, S., and Anderson, A. R. (2008) Change and the development of entrepreneurial networks over time: A processual perspective. *Entrepreneurship Regional Development* 20(2), 125–159.

Johanson, J., and Vahlne, J.-E. (2009) The Uppsala internationalization process model revisited: From liability of foreignness to liability of outsidership. *Journal of International Business Studies* 40, 1411–1431.

Johnstone, H., and Lionais, D. (2004) Depleted communities and community business entrepreneurship: Revaluing space through place. *Entrepreneurship and Regional Development* 16(3), 217–233.

Joireman, S. F. (2017) Ethnic violence, local security and return migration: Enclave communities in Kosovo. *International Migration* 55(5), 122–135.

Judah, T. (2008) *Kosovo: What everyone needs to know.* Oxford University Press, Oxford.

Kalantaridis, C., and Bika, Z. (2006) In-migrant entrepreneurship in rural England: Beyond local embeddedness. *Entrepreneurship and Regional Development* 18, 109–131.

Kellezi, B., Reicher, S., and Cassidy, C. (2009) Surviving the Kosovo conflict: A study of social identity, appraisal of extreme events, and mental well-being. *Applied Psychology* 58(1), 59–83.

Kirzner, I. M. (1973) *Competition and entrepreneurship.* University of Chicago Press, Chicago.

Kirzner, I. M. (1979) *Perception, opportunity and profit: Studies in the theory of entrepreneurship.* University of Chicago Press, Chicago.

Kirzner, I. M. (1982) The theory of entrepreneurship in economic growth. In C. A. Kent, David L. Sexton, and K. H. Vesper (eds.), *Encyclopedia of entrepreneurship.* Prentice Hall, Englewood Cliffs, NJ, pp. 273–276.

Kirzner, I. M. (1985) *Discovery and the capitalist process.* University of Chicago Press, Chicago.

Kirzner, I. M. (1999) Creativity and/or alertness: A reconsideration of the Schumpeterian entrepreneur. *The Review of Austrian Economics* 11(1–2), 5–17.

Kirzner, I. M. (2009) The alert and creative entrepreneur: A clarification. *Small Business Economics* 32(2), 145–152.

Klekowski von Koppenfels, A. (2017) The disinterested state: Negative diasporic policy as an expression of state inclusion and national exclusion. *Journal of Ethnic and Migration Studies* 45(4), 595–612.

Knight, F. (1921) *Risk, uncertainty and profit.* Houghton Mifflin, New York.

Knudsen, R. A. (2010) *Privatization in Kosovo: The International Project 1999–2008.* Center for Security Studies, Zurich.

Koman, M., Lakićević, M., Prašnikar, J., and Svejnar, J. (2015) Asset stripping and firm survival in mass privatization: Testing the Hoff-Stiglitz and Campos-Giovannoni models in Montenegro. *Journal of Comparative Economics* 43(2), 274–289.

Koning, J., and Verver, M. (2013) Historicizing the 'ethnic' in ethnic entrepreneurship: The case of the ethnic Chinese in Bangkok. *Entrepreneurship & Regional Development* 25(5–6), 325–348.

Kosmo, M., and Nedelkoska, L. (2015) *Albanian-American diaspora survey report.* Center for International Development. Harvard University, Boston.

Kosovo Agency for Statistics. (2013) *Study on remittances 2013.* KAS, Pristina.

Krasniqi, B., and Desai, S. (2016) Institutional drivers of high-growth firms: Country-level evidence from 26 transition economies. *Small Business Economics* 47, 1075–1094.

Krasniqi, B. A., and Williams, N. (2018) Migration and intention to return: Entrepreneurial intentions of the diaspora in post-conflict economies. *Post-Communist Economies* 31(4), 464–483.

Krueger, N. (1993) The impact of prior entrepreneurial exposure on perceptions. *Entrepreneurship Theory and Practice* 18(1), 5–22.

Krueger, N., Reilly, M. D., and Carsrud, A. L. (2000) Competing models of entrepreneurial intentions. *Journal of Business Venturing* 15, 411–432.

Kshetri, N. (2013) The diaspora as a change agent in entrepreneurship-related institutions in sub-Saharan Africa. *Journal of Development Entrepreneurship* 18(3), 1–27.

Kveder, C. L. M., and Flahaux, M. L. (2013) Returning to Dakar: A mixed methods analysis of the role of migration experience for occupational status. *World Development* 45, 223–238.

Lajqi, S., and Krasniqi, B. A. (2017) Entrepreneurial growth aspirations in challenging environment: The role of institutional quality, human and social capital. *Strategic Change* 26(4), 385–401.

Lassmann, A., and Busch, C. (2015) Revisiting native and immigrant entrepreneurial activity. *Small Business Economics* 45(4), 841–873.

Lazear, E. P. (2005) Entrepreneurship. *Journal of Labor Economics* 23(4), 649–680.

Leblang, D. (2010) Familiarity breeds investment: Diaspora networks and international investment. *American Political Science Review* 104(3), 584–600.

Ledeneva, 1998). *Russia's economy of favours: Blat, networking, and informal exchange.* Cambridge University Press, New York, NY.

Lee, R., and Jones, O. (2008) Networks, communication and learning during business start-up: The creation of cognitive social capital. *International Small Business Journal* 26(5), 559–594.

Li, C., Isidor, R., Dau, L. A., and Kabst, R. (2017) The more the merrier? Immigrant share and entrepreneurial activities. *Entrepreneurship Theory and Practice* 42(5), 698–733.

Li, H., Zhang, Y., Li, Y., Zhou, L. A., and Zhang, W. (2012) Returnees versus locals: Who perform better in China's technology entrepreneurship? *Strategic Entrepreneurship Journal* 6(3), 257–272.

Liao, J., and Welsch, H. (2005) Roles of social capital in venture creation: Key dimensions and research implications. *Journal of Small Business Management* 43(4), 345–362.

Lin, D., Zheng, W., Lu, J., Liu, X., and Wright, M. (2018) Forgotten or not? Home country embeddedness and returnee entrepreneurship. *Journal of World Business* 54(1), 1–13.

Loxha, A. (2012) *Economic development.* UNDP, Pristina.

Manolova, T. S., and Yan, A. (2002) Institutional constraints and strategic responses of new and small firms in a transforming economy: The case of Bulgaria. *International Small Business Journal* 20(2), 163–184.

Martinez, C., Cummings, M. E., and Vaaler, P. M. (2015) Economic informality and the venture funding impact of migrant remittances to developing countries. *Journal of Business Venturing* 30(4), 526–545.

Mayer, S. D., Harima, A., and Freiling, J. (2015) Network benefits for Ghanaian diaspora and returnee entrepreneurs. *Entrepreneurial Business and Economics Review* 3(3), 95–122.

McCraw, T. K. (2007) *Prophet of innovation: Joseph Schumpeter and creative destruction*. Harvard University Press, Cambridge, MA.

McKeever, E., Jack, S., and Anderson, A. (2015) Embedded entrepreneurship in the creative re-construction of place. *Journal of Business Venturing* 30(1), 50–65.

McKenzie, D. J., and Mistiaen, J. (2009) Surveying migrant households: A comparison of census-based, snowball and intercept point surveys. *Journal of the Royal Statistical Society: Series A (Statistics in Society)* 172(2), 339–360.

McMullen, J. S. (2011) Delineating the domain of development entrepreneurship: A market-based approach to facilitating inclusive economic growth. *Entrepreneurship Theory and Practice* 35(1), 185–215.

Meuleman, M., Jaaskelainen, M., Maula, M. V. J., and Wright, M. (2017) Venturing into the un-known with strangers: Substitutes of relational embeddedness in cross-border partner selec-tion in venture capital syndicates. *Journal of Business Venturing* 32, 131–144.

Michelson, G., Wailes, N., van der Laan, S., and Frost, G. (2004) Ethical investment processes and outcomes. *Journal of Business Ethics* 52(1), 1–10.

Ministry of Foreign Affairs. (2012) *Statistical data on emigrations from Montenegro in the 2nd half of the 20th century*. Ministry of Foreign Affairs, Podgorica.

Ministry of Security. (2016) *Strategy in the area of migrations and asylum and Action Plan for the Period 2016–2020*. Ministry of Security, Sarajevo.

Minniti, M. (2005) Entrepreneurship and network externalities. *Journal of Economic Behavior and Organization* 57(1), 1–27.

Minniti, M., Bygrave, W. D., and Autio, E. (2006) *GEM Global Entrepreneurship Monitor: 2005 executive report*. London Business School, London.

Mollers, J., Meyer, W., Xhema, S., Traikova, D., and Buchenrieder, G. (2015) Cognitive con-structs and the intention to remit. *The Journal of Development Studies* 51(10), 1341–1357.

Moran, P. (2005) Structural vs. relational embeddedness: Social capital and managerial perfor-mance. *Strategic Management Journal* 26(12), 1129–1151.

Mueller, P. (2006) Entrepreneurship in the region: Breeding ground for nascent entrepreneurs? *Small Business Economics* 27(1), 41–58.

Mullings, B. (2011) Diaspora strategies, skilled migrants and human capital enhancement in Jamaica. *Global Networks* 11(1), 24–42.

Murphy, K. M., Shleifer, A., and Vishny, R. W. (1991) The allocation of talent: Implications for growth. *The Quarterly Journal of Economics* 106(2), 503–530.

Newland, K., and Tanaka, H. (2010) *Mobilizing diaspora entrepreneurship for development*. USAID Migration Policy Institute, New York.

Nielsen, T. M., and Riddle, L. (2010) Investing in peace: The motivational dynamics of diaspora investment in post-conflict economies. *Journal of Business Ethics* 89(4), 435–448.

Nikolaev, B., Boudreaux, C. J., and Palich, L. (2018) Cross-country determinants of early-stage necessity and opportunity-motivated entrepreneurship: Accounting for model uncertainty. *Journal of Small Business Management* 56(1), 243–280.

Nkongolo, J., and Chrystostome, E. V. (2013) Engaging diasporas as international entrepreneurs in developing countries: In search of determinants. *Journal of International Entrepreneurship* 11(1), 30–64.

North, D. (1990) *Institutions, institutional change and economic performance*. Cambridge University Press, Cambridge.

Oettl, A., and Agrawal, A. (2008) International labor mobility and knowledge flow external-ities. *Journal of International Business Studies* 39(8), 1242–1260.

Office of the Prime Minister. (2016) *Mobilizing the diaspora for development: Policy note un-derpinning the NDS elaboration process*. Strategic Planning Office of the Office of the Prime Minister, Pristina, Kosovo.

Ojo, S., Nwankwo, S. and Gbandamosi, A. (2013) African diaspora entrepreneurs. Navigating entrepreneurial spaces in 'home' and 'host' countries. *Journal of Entrepreneurship and Innovation* 14(4), 289–299.

Olson, M. (2007) Big bills left on the sidewalk: Why some nations are rich, and others poor. In B. Powell (ed.), *Making poor nations rich: Entrepreneurship and the process of economic development*. Stanford University Press, Stanford, CA, pp. 25–53.

Ostgaard, T., and Birley S. (1996) New venture growth and personal networks. *Journal of Business Research* 36(1), 37–50.

Oviatt, B. M., and McDougall, P. P. (2005) The internationalization of entrepreneurship. *Journal of International Business Studies* 36(1), 2–8.

Parker, S. C. (2004) *The economics of self-employment and entrepreneurship*. Cambridge University Press, Cambridge.

Patel, P. C., and Conklin, B. (2009) The balancing act: The role of transnational habitus and social networks in balancing transnational entrepreneurial activities. *Entrepreneurship Theory and Practice* 33(5), 1045–1078.

Peci, F., Kutllovci, E., Tmava, Q., and Shala, V. (2012) Small and medium enterprises facing institutional barriers in Kosovo. *International Journal of Marketing Studies* 4(1), 95–107.

Pellerin, H., and Mullings, B. (2013) The 'Diaspora option', migration and the changing political economy of development. *Review of International Political Economy* 20(1), 89–120.

Portes, A., and Sensenbrenner, J. (1993) Embeddedness and immigration: Notes on the social determinants of economic action. *American Journal of Sociology* 98(6), 1320–1350.

Pruthi, S., Basu, A., and Wright, M. (2018) Ethnic ties, motivations, and home country entry strategy of transnational entrepreneurs. *Journal of International Entrepreneurship* 16(2), 210–243.

Puffer, S. M., McCarthy, D. J., and Boisot, M. (2010) Entrepreneurship in Russia and China: The impact of formal institutional voids. *Entrepreneurship Theory and Practice* 34(3), 441–467.

Putnam, R. (1995) Bowling alone: America's declining social capital. *Journal of Democracy* 6(1), 65–78.

Qin, F., and Estrin, S. (2015) Does social influence span time and space? Evidence from Indian returnee entrepreneurs. *Strategic Entrepreneurship Journal* 9, 226–242.

Qin, F., Wright, M., and Gao, J. (2017) Are 'sea turtles' slower? Returnee entrepreneurs, venture resources and speed of entrepreneurial entry. *Journal of Business Venturing* 32, 694–706.

Ram, M., and Jones, T. (2008) Ethnic-minority businesses in the UK: A review of research and policy developments. *Environment and Planning C: Government and Policy* 26(2), 352–374.

Ram, M., Jones, T., and Villares-Varela, M. (2016) Migrant entrepreneurship: Reflections on research and practice. *International Small Business Journal* 35(1), 3–18.

Ram, M., Theodorakopoulos, N., and Jones, T. (2008) Forms of capital, mixed embeddedness and Somali enterprise. *Work, Employment and Society* 22(3), 427–446.

Reuber, A. R., Knight, G. A., Liesch, P. W., and Zhou, L. (2018) International entrepreneurship: The pursuit of entrepreneurial opportunities across national borders. *Journal of International Business Studies* 49, 395–406.

Riddle, L., and Brinkerhoff, J. (2011) Diaspora entrepreneurs as institutional change agents: The case of Thamel.com. *International Business Review* 20(6), 670–680.

Riddle, L., Hrivnak, G. A., and Nielsen, T. M. (2010) Transnational diaspora entrepreneurship in emerging markets: Bridging institutional divides. *Journal of International Management* 16(4), 398–411.

Riddle, L., Brinkerhoff, J. M., and Nielsen, T. M. (2008) Partnering to beckon them home: Public-sector innovation for diaspora foreign investment promotion. *Public Administration and Development* 28(1), 54–66.

Romer, P. M. (2007) Economic growth. In D. Henderson (ed.), *The concise encyclopedia of economics*. Liberty Fund, Indianapolis, pp. 128–131.

Rushdie, S. (1992) *Imaginary homelands: Essays and criticism 1981–1991*. Granta, London.

Saar, E., and Unt, M. (2008) Selective mobility into self-employment in post-socialist transition: Early birds, later entrants, quitters and shuttles. *International Small Business Journal* 26(3), 323–349.

Safran, W. (1991) Diasporas in modern societies: Myths of homeland and return. *Diaspora* 1(1), 83–99.

Sanders, M., and Weitzel, U. (2013) Misallocation of entrepreneurial talent in postconflict environments. *Journal of Conflict Resolution* 57(1), 41–64.

Santos, F. M. (2012) A positive theory of social entrepreneurship. *Journal of Business Ethics* 111(3), 335–351.

Sautet, F. (2013) Local and systemic entrepreneurship: Solving the puzzle of entrepreneurship and economic development. *Entrepreneurship Theory and Practice* 37(2), 387–402.

Sautet, F., and Kirzner, I. (2006) *The nature and role of entrepreneurship in markets: Implications for policy*. Policy Primer No. 4, Mercatus Policy Series, George Mason University, Fairfax, VA.

Saxenian, A. (1999) *Silicon Valley's new immigrant entrepreneurs*. Available at http://www.ppic.org/publications/PPIC120/index.html

Saxenian, A. (1996) *Regional advantage: Culture and competition in Silicon Valley and Route 128*. Harvard University Press, Cambridge, MA.

Say, J. B. (2006) *A treatise on political economy*. Scholarly Publishing Office, University of Michigan, Ann Arbor, MI.

Schumpeter, J. A. (1934) *The theory of economic development*. Harvard University Press, Cambridge, MA.

Schumpeter, J. A. (1942) *Capitalism, socialism and democracy*. Routledge, London.

Seabright, P. (2004) *The company of strangers: A natural history of economic life*. Princeton University Press, Princeton, NJ.

Shane, S. (2000) Prior knowledge and the discovery of entrepreneurial opportunities. *Organization Science* 11(4), 448–469.

Shane, S. (2003) *A general theory of entrepreneurship: The individual–opportunity nexus*. Edward Elgar, Cheltenham, UK.

Shane, S. (2009) Why encouraging more people to become entrepreneurs is bad public policy. *Small Business Economics* 31(2), 141–149.

Shepherd, D. A. (2004) Educating entrepreneurship students about emotion and learning from failure. *Academy of Management Learning and Education* 3(3), 274–287.

Simmie, J., and Martin, R. (2009) The economic resilience of regions: Towards an evolutionary approach. *Cambridge Journal of Regions, Economy and Society* 3(1), 27–43.

Sinatti, G., and Horst, C. (2015) Migrants as agents of development: Diaspora engagement discourse and practice in Europe. *Ethnicities* 15(1), 134–149.

Sistek, F., and Dimitrovova, B. (2003) National minorities in Montenegro after the break-up of Yugoslavia. In F. Bieber (ed.), *Montenegro in transition: Problems of identity and statehood*. Nomos, Baden-Baden, pp. 159–179.

Smallbone, D., Kitching, D., and Athayde, R. (2010) Ethnic diversity, entrepreneurship and competitiveness in a global city. *International Small Business Journal* 28(2), 174–190.

Smallbone, D., and Welter, F. (2001) The distinctiveness of entrepreneurship in transition economies. *Small Business Economics* 16(1), 249–262.

Smallbone, D., and Welter, F. (2004) Entrepreneurship in transition economies: Necessity or opportunity driven? www.babson.edu/entrep/fer/BABSON2003/XXV/XXV-S8/xxv-s8.htm

Snyder, C. R., and Lopez, S. J. (2007) *Positive psychology: The scientific and practical explorations of human strengths*. Sage, Thousand Oaks, CA.

Sobel, R. S. (2008) Testing Baumol: Institutional quality and the productivity of entrepreneurship. *Journal of Business Venturing* 23(6), 641–655.

Sobel, R. S., Clark, J. R., and Lee, D. R. (2007) Freedom, barriers to entry, entrepreneurship, and economic progress. *The Review of Austrian Economics* 20(4), 221–236.

Solow, R. (1956) A contribution to the theory of economic growth. *Quarterly Journal of Economics* 70(1), 65–94.

Sorensen, J. B. (2007) Closure vs. exposure: mechanisms in the intergenerational transmission of self-employment. In M. Ruef and M. Lounsbury (eds.), *Research in the sociology of organizations*. Elsevier/JAI, New York, NY, pp. 83–124.

Spencer, J., and Gomez, C. (2004) The relationship among national institutional structures, economic factors, and domestic entrepreneurial activity: A multi-country study. *Journal of Business Research* 57, 1098–1107.

Stark, O. (2004) Rethinking brain drain. *World Development* 32(1), 15–22.

Storey, D. J. (1991) The birth of new firms: Does unemployment matter? A review of the evidence. *Small Business Economics* 3(3), 167–178.

Storey, D. J. (1994) *Understanding the small business sector*. Thomson Learning, London.

Swedberg, R. (2000) *Entrepreneurship: The social science view*. Oxford University Press, Oxford.

The Economist. (2013) *Returning students: Plight of the Sea Turtles*. https://www.economist.com/china/2013/07/06/plight-of-the-sea-turtles

Thompson, E. R. (2009) Individual entrepreneurial intent: Construct clarification and development of an internationally reliable metric. *Entrepreneurship Theory and Practice* 33(3), 669–694.

Thurik, A., Carree, M. A., van Stel, A., and Audretsch, D. B. (2008) Does self-employment reduce unemployment? *Journal of Business Venturing* 23(6), 673–686.

Tonoyan, V., Strohmeyer, R., Habib, M., and Perlitz, M. (2010) Corruption and entrepreneurship: How formal and informal institutions shape small firm behavior in transition and mature market economies. *Entrepreneurship Theory and Practice* 34(5), 803–832.

Transparency International. (2019) *Corruption perceptions index 2018*. Transparency International, Berlin.

Turner, T. (2010) The jobs immigrants do: Issues of displacement and marginalisation in the Irish labour market. *Work, Employment and Society* 24(2), 318–336.

Turnock, D. (2001) Location trends for foreign direct investment in East Central Europe. *Environment and Planning C: Government and Policy* 19(6), 849–880.

Turok, I. (2004) Cities, regions and competitiveness. *Regional Studies* 38(9), 1069–1083.

UNHCR. (2018) *Global trends: Forced displacement in 2018*. UNCHR, Geneva.

United Nations. (2020) *International migration report 2020*. UN, New York.

United Nations Development Programme. (2012) *Kosovo remittance study 2012*. UNDP, Pristina.

United Nations Development Programme. (2014) *Kosovo human development report 2014: Migration as a force for development*. UNDP, Pristina.

Uzzi, B. (1997) Social structure and competition in interfirm networks: The paradox of embeddedness. *Administrative Science Quarterly* 42(1), 35–67.

Vaaler, P. M. (2011) Immigrant remittances and the venture investment environment of developing countries. *Journal of International Business Studies* 42(9), 1121–1149.

Vaaler, P. M. (2013) Diaspora concentration and the venture investment impact of remittances. *Journal of International Management* 19(1), 26–46.

Van de Laar, M., and de Neubourg, C. (2006) Emotions and foreign direct investment: A theoretical and empirical exploration. *Management International Review* 46(1), 207–233.

Verheul I., Wennekers S., Audretsch D., Thurik R. (2002) An eclectic theory of entrepreneurship: Policies, institutions and culture. In D. Audretsch, R. Thurik, I, Verheul, and

S. Wennekers (eds.), *Entrepreneurship: Determinants and policy in a European-US comparison*. Economics of Science, Technology and Innovation, vol. 27. Springer, Boston, MA, pp. 11–81.

Vershinina, N., Barrett, R., and Meyer, M. (2011) Forms of capital, intra-ethnic variation and Polish entrepreneurs in Leicester. *Work, Employment and Society* 25(1), 101–117.

Vorley, T., and Williams, N. (2016a) Between petty corruption and criminal extortion: How entrepreneurs in Bulgaria and Romania operate within a devil's circle. *International Small Business Journal* 34(6), 797–817.

Vorley, T., and Williams, N. (2016b) Fostering entrepreneurship and economic growth: Pathways to economic resilience in Kosovo. *World Review of Entrepreneurship, Management and Sustainable Development* 13(2–3), 159–177.

Waldinger, R. (2015) *The cross-border connection: Immigrants, emigrants and their homelands.* Harvard University Press, Cambridge, MA.

Wang, Q., and Liu, C. Y. (2015) Transnational activities of immigrant-owned firms and their performances in the USA. *Small Business Economics* 44(2), 345–390.

Weinar, A. (2010) Instrumentalising diasporas for development: International and European policy discourses. In R. Baubock and T. Faist (eds.), *Diaspora and transnationalism: Concepts, theories and methods.* Amsterdam University Press, Amsterdam, pp. 73–90.

Weinar, A. (2017) From emigrants to free movers: Whither European emigration and diaspora policy? *Journal of Ethnic and Migration Studies* 43(13), 2228–2246.

Welpe, I. M., Sporrle, M., Grichnik, D., Michl, T., and Audretsch, D. B. (2012) Emotions and opportunities: The interplay of opportunity evaluation, fear, joy, and anger as antecedent of entrepreneurial exploitation. *Entrepreneurship Theory and Practice* 36(1), 69–96.

Welter, F., and Smallbone, D. (2011) Institutional perspectives on entrepreneurial behaviour in challenging environments. *Journal of Small Business Management* 49(1), 107–125.

Welter, F., Baker, T., Audretsch, D. B., and Gartner, W. B. (2017a) Everyday entrepreneurship: A call for entrepreneurship research to embrace entrepreneurial diversity. *Entrepreneurship Theory and Practice* 41(3), 311–321.

Welter, F., Xheneti, M., and Smallbone, D. (2017b) Entrepreneurial resourcefulness in unstable institutional contexts: The example of European Union borderlands. *Strategic Entrepreneurship Journal* 12(1), 23–53.

Wennekers, S., and Thurik, A. R. (1999) Linking entrepreneurship and economic growth. *Small Business Economics* 13(1), 27–55.

Werker, C., and Athreye, S. (2004) Marshall's disciples: Knowledge and innovation driving regional economic development and growth. *Journal of Evolutionary Economics* 14(5), 505–523.

Westlund, H., and Bolton, R. (2003) Local social capital and entrepreneurship. *Small Business Economics* 21(2), 77–133.

Williams, N. (2018) Mobilising diaspora to promote homeland investment: The progress of policy in post-conflict economies. *Environment and Planning C; Politics and Space* 36(7), 1256–1279.

Williams, N. (2020) Moving beyond remittances: The evolution of diaspora policy in post-conflict economies. *International Small Business Journal* 38(1), 41–62.

Williams, N., and Efendic, A. (2019) Internal displacement and external migration in a post-conflict context: Perceptions of institutions by migrant entrepreneurs. *Journal of International Entrepreneurship* 17, 558–585.

Williams, N., and Krasniqi, B. (2018) Coming out of conflict: The impact of international experience on the entrepreneurial activity of migrants. *Journal of International Entrepreneurship* 16(2), 301–323.

Williams, N., and Vorley, T. (2014) Economic resilience and entrepreneurship: Lessons from the Sheffield City Region. *Entrepreneurship and Regional Development* 26(3–4), 257–281.

Williams, N., and Vorley, T. (2015) Institutional asymmetry: How formal and informal institutions affect entrepreneurship in Bulgaria. *International Small Business Journal* 33(8), 840–861.

Williams, N., and Vorley, T. (2017) Creating institutional alignment and fostering productive entrepreneurship in new born states. *Entrepreneurship and Regional Development* 29(5–6), 444–446.

Williams, N., Vorley, T., and Williams, C. C. (2017a) *Entrepreneurship and institutions: The causes and consequences of institutional asymmetry*. Rowman and Littlefield, London.

Williams, N., Radevic, D. Gherhes, C., and Vorley, T. (2017b) Corruption and entrepreneurship in new born states: Some lessons from Montenegro. *South East European Journal of Economics and Business* 12(2), 31–45.

Williams, N., and Williams, C. C. (2012) Evaluating the socio-spatial contingency of entrepreneurial motivations: A case study of English deprived urban neighbourhoods. *Entrepreneurship and Regional Development* 24(7–8), 661–684.

Williamson, C. R. (2009) Informal institutions rule: Institutional arrangements and economic performance. *Public Choice* 139(3–4), 371–387.

Williamson, O. E. (2000) The new institutional economics: Taking stock, looking ahead. *Journal of Economic Literature* 38(3), 595–613.

Winiecki, J. (2001) Formal rules, informal rules and economic performance. *Acta Oeconomica* 51(2), 147–172.

World Bank. (2000) *World development report, 2000–2001*. World Bank, Washington, DC.

World Bank. (2011) *Migration and economic development in Kosovo*, Report No. 60590—XK. World Bank, Washington, DC.

World Bank. (2016) *Migration and development*. World Bank, Washington, DC.

World Bank. (2018) *Moving for prosperity: Global migration and labor markets*. World Bank, Washington, DC.

World Bank. (2019) *Doing business*. World Bank, Washington, DC.

Wright, M., Liu, X., Buck, T., and Filatotchev, I. (2008) Returnee entrepreneurs, science park location choice, and performance: An analysis of high-technology SMEs in China. *Entrepreneurship Theory and Practice* 32(1), 131–155.

Xheneti, M., and Kitching, J. (2011) From discourse to implementation: Enterprise policy development in postcommunist Albania. *Environment and Planning C: Government and Policy* 29(6), 1018–1036.

Xheneti, M., Smallbone, D., and Welter, F. (2013) EU enlargement effects on cross-border informal entrepreneurial activities. *European Urban and Regional Studies* 20(3), 314–328.

Yannis, A. (2009) The politics and geopolitics of the status of Kosovo: The circle is never round. *Southeast European and Black Sea Studies* 9(1–2), 161–170.

Zaheer, S. (1995) Overcoming the liability of foreignness. *Academy of Management Journal* 38, 341–363.

Zahra, S. A., Gedajlovic, E., Neubaum, D. O., and Shulman, J. M. (2009) A typology of social entrepreneurs: Motives, search processes and ethical challenges. *Journal of Business Venturing* 24(5), 519–32.

Zaiceva, A., and Zimmermann, K. F. (2016) Returning home at times of trouble? Return migration of EU enlargement migrants during the crisis. In M. Kahanec and K.F. Zimmermann (eds.), *Labor migration, EU enlargement, and the Great Recession*. Springer, Berlin Heidelberg, pp. 397–418.

Zheng, C., and Musteen, M. (2018) The impact of remittances on opportunity-based and necessity-based entrepreneurial activities. *Academy of Entrepreneurship Journal* 24(3), 1–13.

Zhou, W. (2013) Political connections and entrepreneurial investment: Evidence from China's transition economy. *Journal of Business Venturing* 28(2), 299–315.

Zivin, J. G., and Small, A. (2005) A Modigliani-Miller theory of altruistic corporate social status responsibility. *Topics in Economic Analysis & Policy* 5, 1–19.

Index